Mind
Our Greatest Gift

THE *Mananam* SERIES

(*Mananam*–Sanskrit for "Reflection upon the Truth")

The Choice is Yours
Solitude
Vedanta in Action
The Mystery of Creation
Self-Discovery
Beyond Sorrow
On the Path
The Pursuit of Happiness
The Question of Freedom
Harmony and Beauty
The Razor's Edge
The Essential Teacher

(continued on inside back page)

Other Chinmaya Publication Series:

THE *Self-Discovery* SERIES

Meditation and Life
by Swami Chinmayananda

Self-Unfoldment
by Swami Chinmayananda

THE *Hindu Culture* SERIES

Hindu Culture: An Introduction
by Swami Tejomayananda

THE *Mananam* SERIES

Mind
Our Greatest Gift

CHINMAYA PUBLICATIONS

Chinmaya Publications
Chinmaya Mission West Publications Division
Main Office
P.O. Box 129
Piercy, CA 95587, USA

Chinmaya Publications
Chinmaya Mission West Publications Division
Distribution Office
560 Bridgetown Pike
Langhorne, PA 19053, USA
Phone: (215) 396-0390   Fax: (215) 396-9710
Toll Free: 1-888-CMW-READ (1-888-269-7323)

Central Chinmaya Mission Trust
Sandeepany Sadhanalaya
Saki Vihar Road
Mumbai, India 400 072

First Printing 1995
Second Printing 1998

Credits:

Series Editors: Margaret Leuverink, Br. Rajeshwar
Associate Editor: Lalita Shenoy
Cover design: Dawn Canadian, Inc.
Cover photogragh: Swami Siddhananda
Inside photographs: Treehouse Digital Studio

Library of Congress Catalog Card Number 95-70524

ISBN 1-880687-09-7

Contents

Preface

"Bring your mind to where your hands are at every moment." With this one sentence Swami Chinmayananda has summarized all of the ancient Vedic teachings. The entire thrust of these teachings is that of mastering the mind. Our mind can cause us much suffering but it is also the means of attaining the greatest happiness. To gain this happiness, however, we must first understand the mind and bring it under our control.

All powerful instruments come equipped with an operating manual. The benevolent Creator also left us with operating instructions—which are enshrined in the scriptures of all major religions. Spiritual disciplines such as prayer, worship, and selfless actions help purify and quiet the mind. A quiet, alert mind is highly effective and becomes receptive to Self-knowledge. This is confirmed by the authors in this book as they show how a well-trained mind can bring true happiness and freedom.

Swami Chinmayananda, the renowned Vedantic Master, begins Part One, "A Gift from God," by pointing out that just as a river consists of the flow of water, the mind consists of the flow of thoughts. He explains that ignorance of our true nature causes all thought-agitations, and how three different thought-textures keep us from knowing our true Self. In the following three articles we come to see the preciousness of the gift that we have been given. Swami Jyotirmayananda of the Yoga Research Foundation writes that we can show our gratitude for the gift by making good use of it. He also reveals practices and attitudes necessary to reach the goal of Self-realization. Swami Chidananda, head of the Divine Life Society, assures us that our mind can become our best friend. Swami Satchidananda of the Integral Yoga Institute concludes this section by clarifying the words "self-love" and "self-judgment" and shows us that the greatest Comforter is within us.

Part Two, "Using the Gift Wisely," focuses on development of the mind. The contemporary writers Ram Dass and Stephen Levine start this section by writing that discriminative awareness helps us keep the proper goal in view. This awareness consists of knowing that "all of life's experiences are needed for us to awaken to our higher nature." Yogi Ramacharaka of the Yoga Foundation demonstrates how the use of mental imagery can help us build character. Swami Vivekananda then states that systematic development of the mind includes the ability to concentrate and detach the mind at will. Luella Cole writes that a mature attitude consists of the ability to accept people as they are, faults and all.

The American writer Jules Willing, who developed an interest in writing and teaching after retiring from a successful career in personnel management and training, encourages us to respect our minds by paying due attention to our thoughts. Swami Chinmayananda ends this part by pointing out that to achieve anything in life we need sincerity and involvement, and this is also required to rise above the mind.

The ancient masters have understood the inherent power of the mind for centuries. How this power can be utilized is the theme of Part Three, "A Powerful Tool." Paramahansa Yogananda of the Self-Realization Fellowship illustrates the power of thoughts when he describes how his guru became ill or healthy depending on the thought-suggestions given to him by his teacher. Jayesh Nishar, a medical student at the time of writing this article, proves how our attitudes help us in getting well. Vimala Thakar, a former student of J. Krishnamurti and renowned teacher, then shows that memories of the past prevent us from relating to others in "fresh and innocent ways," and that transcendence of the mind is effortless once we understand it.

As our discrimination develops and we overcome the delusion that worldly objects bring happiness, we begin "Reveling Within" which is the main focus of Part Four. The contemporary sage Ramana Maharshi encourages us to persistently inquire into our true nature by asking the question "Who am I." Swami Chinmayananda continues this theme by saying that we can maintain the natural serenity of the mind without effort when we no longer "imagificate." The Buddhist teacher and writer Sogyal Rinpoche encourages us to develop a compassionate attitude toward our "family" of thoughts, and points out various pitfalls during meditation. Swami Chinmayananda then presents helpful hints and attitudes necessary for contemplation. In the final article, Swami Ranganathananda of the Ramakrishna Mission emphasizes what devotees have known all along, that total surrender and love for the Lord can lead us quickly to the Highest.

Thus we see what a great gift the mind is when it is properly developed and utilized. It is this achievement alone that can provide us with lasting peace and happiness. We need not run to the Himalayas, nor practice rigid austerities. By fulfilling our daily obligations, full of love and enthusiasm, along with discriminative awareness, we can attain the highest goal. There are as many paths to the goal as there are minds. The greatest gift is the one that takes us completely by surprise. Once our thoughts are clear, we will discover, to our great delight, their innate creativity, and transcending them is only a step away.

The Editors

PART ONE

A Gift from God

What lies behind us,
and what lies before us,
are tiny matters,
compared to what lies within us.

Ralph Waldo Emerson

Taking the name of Kali, dive deep down, O mind,
Into the heart's fathomless depths,
Where many a precious gem lies hid.
But never believe the bed of the ocean bare of gems
If the first few dives you fail;
With firm resolve and self-control
Dive deep and make your way to Mother Kali's realm.
Down in the ocean depth of heavenly Wisdom lie
The wondrous pearls of Peace, O mind;
And you yourself can gather them.
If you but have pure love
And follow the scriptures' rule.

Within those ocean depths, as well,
Six alligators lurk—lust, anger, and the rest
(avarice, delusion, pride, and envy)
Swimming about in search of prey.
Smear yourself with the turmeric of discrimination;
The very smell of it will shield you from their jaws.
Upon the ocean bed lies strewn,
Unnumbered pearls and precious gems;
Plunge in, says Ramprasad,
and gather up handfuls there.

Sri Ramakrishna
The Gospel of Sri Ramakrishna

I

Understanding the Mind

by Swami Chinmayananda

The importance of understanding the mind cannot be emphasized enough; our entire evolutionary progress depends on it. It is the mind that determines the quality and nature of all that we experience in life. Thus, to control and develop the mind is the secret of all personality development. Mastery over the situations in life without a mastery over the mind can only be a vain dream. But in order to gain this mastery, we must first understand the mind.

When we are asked to define the mind, we usually say that the mind is thoughts—for when there are thoughts we consider that the mind exists, and when there are no thoughts we say that there is no mind. Thoughts and the mind are very much interrelated. If the thoughts are agitated, the mind is agitated. If the thoughts are hopeful, the mind is hopeful. The mind is as the thoughts in it. However, thought alone is not the mind. The sages of India concluded that thoughts and the mind have a relationship similar to that of water and the river.

A river is not just water, nor can it be said that it is water with two banks. A river exists only when water is flowing. Thus, *flowing* is the essence of the river. Similarly, thoughts are not the mind. But thoughts flowing one after another in an unbroken continuity create a delusory "something" called the mind. And this mind at times persecutes us with its low animal urges, and at other times leads us with its higher demands of divine urges.

The Knots of the Heart

When there is least agitation of thought we are in a maximum state of happiness. The stormier the flood of thoughts, the more disturbed the mind becomes and we find ourselves plunged into a state of painful agitation.

The mind becomes calm through a process of stilling the thoughts. Unfortunately, this is not easy for us because of the presence of what is known in Vedanta as the "knots of the heart." The sages used this term not in a physical sense but to indicate that there is a three-pronged process which binds us to the lower realms of discord and unhappiness. These three knots are: ignorance, desire, and action.

If only we could be fully aware of our all-perfect, omnipotent, omniscient nature! But ignorance of our real spiritual identity creates a feeling of imperfection within us. The revolt against this sense of imperfection manifests itself as desires at the mental level. When desires open up the volcano peaks of the mind they throw out a scorching lava of thought-currents. Without desire, no thought can arise. And when a desire becomes fully established in the mind, in the onward flow of thoughts generated by it, that very desire expresses itself as actions in the outer world.

Thus, ignorance at the spiritual level itself is desire rising in the mental level, and desires are then amplified in the grosser sense-world of objects as actions. The grossness or divinity of our actions are expressions of the quality and nature of our desires, which, in turn, advertise the degree and depth of our ignorance.

All spiritual practices are scientific techniques that help

purify, strengthen, and direct the activities of the mind toward removing ignorance of our true nature. With the end of this ignorance, eternal Knowledge comes to shine forth in the final destination of evolution—Self-realization.

II

The Three Veils of Thought

by Swami Chinmayananda

We are essentially divine, but the divinity in us is covered by a veil of thoughts. The differences in these thoughts give rise to the variety of human beings we see in the world. The textbooks of Vedanta delineate three types of thought textures, or *guṇas*, through which the human mind functions:

Sattva—purity: thoughts that are pure and noble.

Rajas—passion: thoughts that are passionate and agitated.

Tamas—inertia: thoughts that are dull and inactive.

These thought textures, in various permutations, determine individual personalities. And on any given day or during any hour, one of these three textures may play the predominant role in each of us.

Before we fully awaken in the morning, when we feel sluggish and sleepy, we are under the influence of the *tamasic* texture of thought.

During a busy day at the office, *rajas* plays a more significant role in defining the texture of our thoughts.

As we listen to a talk on the wisdom of the *Bhagavad Gītā*, a *sattvic* mood may permeate our mind.

Sattva is the subtlest of the three *guṇas*. It is the state of mind filled with equanimity, serenity, and creative poise and therefore best suited for contemplation of the Higher. *Rajas* is the condition of the mind when it is agitated, stormy, ambitious, riddled with overpowering desires, bursting with emotions, and restless with desire-prompted activities. *Tamas* is the state of mind in complete inertia, filled with indolence and carelessness, it describes a condition that reveals no consistency of purpose, amiability of emotions, or nobility in actions.

Sattva

Each of these thought textures, even *sattva*, is a form of bondage. As the *Bhagavad Gītā* says:

Sattva *binds by attachment to happiness and knowledge.*
(Bhagavad Gītā XIV:6)

Because a *sattvic* mind is purified of the agitations of *rajas* and cleansed of the indolence of *tamas*, it allows us to experience a greater share of inner peace and subtler understanding. However, even a *sattvic* mind is attached to the world of objects-emotions-thoughts and is therefore denied the higher joy of the Self. A golden chain, if sufficiently strong, can also bind us as any iron chain can.

After we have experienced the joys of creative thinking or the inspiring life of goodness and wisdom, we may become so attached to them that we will sacrifice anything in order to consistently experience those subtler joys.

A scientist working with total dedication in her laboratory; a painter working at his canvas in his drafty studio; a poet unaccepted by society, living in public parks while seeking his own inner joy from his visions and words; martyrs facing cruel persecutions; politicians suffering long years of exile—all experience the joy of living in a *sattvic* mood.

These are all examples of how people who have experienced the subtler thrills of a *sattvic* mind become bound to their joy-bearing activities, just as much as others who become bound to the thrills of material satisfaction.

Rajas

When we experience an onslaught of *rajasic* influences in the mind, it is choked with a hundred tormenting passions, which express themselves in a variety of urges, desires, and emotions. Once the *rajasic* person fulfills a desire, the next desire is not far behind, robbing him of the experience of any peace and joy. The *rajasic* person, always anxious to have more, can never keep quiet. He acts on endlessly—earning and spending, saving and protecting. Either anxious to have more or fearing to lose what he has gained, he is whipped onward from action to action.

Tamas

Under the influence of *tamas*, our capacity to discriminate between right and wrong is veiled. *Tamas* binds us to our lower nature by providing us with endless misconceptions about the true purpose of life, which leads to a life of indolence and heedlessness. If a person is to leave behind his *tamasic* life, he must first whip up his *tamas* with *rajas* and then evolve further into *sattva*.

We can summarize the differences between the three *guṇas* as follows:

Sattva gives the appearance of seeming inactivity but in reality is characterized by maximum activity; it may be likened to a fan revolving at such a tremendous speed that its motion is not perceptible. A great poet or thinker absorbed all the time in deep contemplation is *sattvic* in nature.

Rajas typifies activity similar to a fan in motion. A passionate youth bristling with activity is *rajasic* in nature.

Tamas is the quality of mind that can be compared to a motionless fan. An idler who wastes all his time in laziness and sleep is *tamasic*.

Covers of the Self

Each of the thought textures creates a different veil over our true nature, the pure Self. The *Bhagavad Gītā* uses three striking analogies to describe these veilings:

Sattvic desires veil the Self like smoke covering the fire. Even a passing breeze can remove the smoke. Similarly, a little prayer or meditation can remove *sattvic* desires.

Rajasic desires cover the Self like dust on a mirror. In this case, some effort is necessary to wipe off the dust. The various religious practices and paths in *vāsanā* exhaustion teach us how to get rid of such desires.

The pure Self is enveloped in *tamasic* desires like a fetus in the womb. Such desires cannot be removed easily or without much effort. Evolution from this stage involves time and patience, just as a fetus needs to evolve to a fully grown baby to emerge out of the womb.

The three *guṇas* are expressions of the ignorance of our true nature, the pure Self. One who has "crossed over the *guṇas*," as the *Bhagavad Gītā* says (Chapter XIV), has transcended the mind-intellect equipment and is no longer affected by any mental condition. He lives in the infinite joys of the Self. To him, the ordinary vehicles of joy and sorrow can no longer supply any special quota of experience. Ever steady and balanced, such a Self-realized person lives beyond the storms of the mind, ever peaceful and blissful.

III

The Highest Discipline

by Swami Jyotirmayananda

The greatest gift that God has given you is your mind. This incredible instrument, if used correctly, gives you the capacity to reason, think, and feel in a way that sets humanity apart from the limitations of the animal kingdom. Take the human mind away, and the world sinks in darkness. It is through the mind that we recognize the world with its complexity, its beauty, and its majesty. Who knows the mountains as mountains? Who enjoys the rivers and has given names to them? Who has explored the mysteries of the universe? It is the human mind, not the instinct-dominated mind of the animal, that has given names, designations, and attributes to things. For that most wonderful instrument of mind you must be profoundly grateful.

That gratitude must be expressed through a sincere effort to use the mind to its fullest capacity. Sometimes we receive a great book as a gift, thank the person heartily, and then put it up on a bookshelf where it may sit untouched for years. Reading the book and benefiting from its wisdom would have been a better "thank you" to the giver. Likewise, God has given the gift of mind, but if you waste your mental energy in idleness, in negative thinking, or by worrying over trifles day by day, you are failing to express your gratitude to the divine Giver in a meaningful way.

It is said in the Upanishads, "Mind is the cause of bondage and release." Through the mind you can ascend to the sublimest heights of prosperity or descend to the lowest depths of degradation; so amazing is the power of your mind that it can take you from overwhelming joy to gripping sorrow in a matter of minutes.

Through yoga philosophy you learn that your mind, which has existed throughout all your countless embodiments, molds your body. This truth may seem confusing because most people equate "mind" with the brain and nervous system. However, this is an erroneous way of thinking. Just as electricity is different from the wires through which it flows, so too, mind is different from the brain and nervous system through which it flows.

Making Your Own Destiny

Prior to your birth, mind was there. Owing to the mysterious operation of karma, the mind chooses your body. It has created the circumstances that have placed you in your present family. All the situations of your life are a result of the karmic impressions within your mind—because of this, every situation has a purpose leading to your evolution.

Many people do not understand this point, believing that the developments in their lives are accidental. Many, having studied about genetics in school, feel that the laws of heredity explain everything about why they look and behave as they do. When viewing any deficiencies or accomplishments in their personality they say that they are probably due to the genes that, say, their grandfather passed to them. But this is not so. According to yoga philosophy, it is karma that has led you to your family and that arranges all the hereditary factors, making them fall into place to create your realities.

Furthermore, the fundamental truth of karma is that you create it each second you live. In the past you consciously allowed your mind to move in a particular way. As a result of it karma was formed, which has now created your body. You may ask, "If mind creates everything, why does a person choose painful situations? Why does a person choose to be miserable, to be born in a poor family, or to be born in one with many adversities?"

Let me give you a simple explanation with this illustration. Suppose you are blind in both eyes and pray to God, "O Lord, give me at least one eye to see with." So you die as a blind man and then are reborn as a one-eyed man. From your very childhood people laugh at you. In your unhappiness you cry out, "O God, why did you put me in this miserable state? You are a cruel God," and you develop many frustrations.

The same applies to your real life in a more intricate way. You have promoted everything that you experience. To most people this idea is shocking, but rather, it should be most inspiring because you know that your entire life has been placed in your own hands. As long as you feel that your life is in someone else's hands, whose moods you do not know, you cannot be at rest.

But yoga philosophy explains that your life is in your own hands. You are the cause of whatever has evolved in your personality and in the circumstances of your life, be they good or bad, positive or negative. Therefore, you have the freedom to change your situation, to mold your destiny according to your will and reason.

So powerful a tool is there in the hands of the soul that by using one's mind, one can attain the highest. But for most people the highest cannot be envisioned; human aspiration is very shallow. Coming back to the blind man, all he wanted was to have one eye. He did not care whether he was born in a poor family or whether he had to endure miserable situations. The only thing that was important to him at the time was to have vision in one eye.

Let me give you another instance of mind's magic. In ancient times ascetics, persons practicing intense austerity, would wander about the countryside begging for food. One such ascetic knocked on the door of a house hoping that the lady of the house would give him food. When she had done so, he said, "I am highly pleased. I shall bless you. May you become the mother of five sons."

The woman became extremely angry, saying, "Five sons! Why, I already have ten sons. What is this, a blessing or a curse?"

So you see that the ascetic's mind was limited in its understanding. Similarly, sometimes when you think you are blessing yourself you are actually cursing yourself, because your soul has much more possibility than your mind desires.

Pursuit of the Highest Goal

Instead of desiring things and going after them, you should quietly explore your mind and allow it to unfold to its outer limits; that is, place before your mind the goal of Self-realization. Do not let ordinary desires guide your mental process because no matter what your desires may be you are cursing yourself— you are placing limitations before yourself, and no desire will lead you to the highest. The highest "desire" that should captivate your mind is the aspiration for Self-realization, when all your mental resources are explored and well utilized.

A human being uses only a fragment of his mind in one lifetime. The mind can be compared to a great iceberg: nine-tenths of it lies submerged, while only a tiny portion is visible above the surface of the water. And in the case of human beings, that which is revealed—the conscious mind—is continually being put under tremendous stress and tension over the most trivial matters. Such is the sad predicament of human beings.

The most important step in working with and controlling your mind is to gain the keen insight that your goal is Self-realization. When you become Self-realized, you are no longer dependent upon the body, the mind, the senses, or the ego. You are not individualized; you become universal, one with God. In the state of Self-realization all the desires of the mind are satisfied.

Two Levels of Mind

As you strive to control the mind it is important to understand that you are dealing with the mind on two levels—conscious and unconscious. The conscious mind is the mind that you know when you are awake. The unconscious represents a vast aspect of the mind that you do not know, and its workings play a great part in your life.

Because the unconscious affects you in a way that is powerful yet hard to fathom, you must be patient as you work to build happiness and joy in your life, and cultivate positive qualities in your personality. Suppose you decide to practice positive thinking for a few days, believing that everything is going to be rosy and sweet. Then, when you find that your optimistic view is not working out, you become frustrated. You should not be frustrated or discouraged, however, because your effort has affected your unconscious for the better—and it continues to do so.

Spiritual Practices

There are some well-evolved techniques that sages have devised for helping one to handle the unconscious. Let me give you a few of these. The most important is the practice of meditation. Early in the morning, sit quietly and watch your mind. Train yourself to concentrate so that you may enter into the meditative state easily. As you practice day by day, you create new grooves or impressions in your unconscious. Consequently, you bring about a profound change in your personality.

The next is *japa*, which is repetition of a divine name or of a brief prayer that helps your mind build positive impressions. *Japa* is the most effective way of overcoming stress, pain, suffering, and frustration because it allows your mind to become aware of the divine presence and feel you are in touch with God.

When you begin to deeply feel that God is guiding you at all times, you become relaxed in any situation. You are no longer frightened by the unknown, nor frustrated when you see that developments in your life cannot be controlled by your ego. Developing that attitude of surrender is a great art. Whatever you do physically or mentally, feel that you are offering it to the God within you. So meditation, prayer, and adapting a spirit of surrender in daily life are all powerful processes for changing your unconscious.

Vigilance is of utmost importance in one's daily life. Watch your mind just as you do the objects in the world. Preserve your mental health as you would your favorite possessions. Most people do not value their mental health and stability; they are far more interested in the objects that clutter their lives. This is a strange predicament that is due to ignorance.

When you are alone, facing your own internal life, you should practice meditation and *japa*. Relax with a spirit of surrender and study scriptures that elevate your mind. Never let your mind go off on a negative tangent. Generally, whenever people are upset, they sit with negative thoughts churning in the mind hour after hour; and such thinking goes on generating its impression in the unconscious, reducing their willpower and weakening their minds.

If you see that you are overcome by negativity when you are alone, then you should take recourse to some kind of *satsanga* or good association with others in a setting where spiritual teachings are being given, or you should be involved in work that takes you out of the negative aspect of mind.

When you are interacting with others, you must evolve the art of adapting and adjusting to the people around you. In daily life, you come into contact with many different kinds of people, so you need to watch your mind as you react to them. This process of watching your mind with great vigilance is the greatest *sādhana* (spiritual practice) that one can perform.

Most spiritual practitioners develop an eccentric view of *sādhana* and feel that if they get up early and do their meditation, *japa*, and other similar practices, then they have done all they need to do in the name of *sādhana*. What difference does it make if they shout at or hurt other people's feelings, and never try to be adaptable?

Such people do not give importance to the art of adaptability because of the erroneous idea that *sādhana* and practical life are completely separated from each other. But this is not so. If you aspire to attain God-realization, to control your mind, then the world is your testing ground. What you accomplish within yourself is tested every day in God's examination hall.

Suppose, for example, that early in the morning during your meditation you recognize the great beauty of humility and vow that you will be humble from then on, but later in the day, someone accidentally steps on your toes, causing you to lose your temper. Or someone praises you for doing a good job and this makes your head swell. Thus in the examination hall of daily life, when you see your ego being easily jarred by pleasure and pain, you realize that you have not yet become humble and you move onward with renewed effort.

When you see that you have failed in the practice of a virtue, you need not develop a sense of regret or repentance. Rather, simply look at your mind just as you would a malfunctioning computer or dishwasher and say, "Where has it gone wrong?" And you practice it again and again with increased vigilance until that virtuous quality is established in your personality.

Helpful Attitudes

The scriptures speak of four attitudes that one ought to adopt in dealing with other people. First, when you encounter people who are your peers, be friendly toward them. Refrain from developing jealousy toward or gossiping about them. Do not search for some defect in your neighbor's life-style or personality that can make him look bad in everyone's eyes. When you find some mistakes in a person it gives you a kind of satisfaction. But that is the wrong way to use your mind. If your neighbor acquires a lot of money or attains some kind of success, do not feel, "I should have gotten that success. Why is it that he gets all that and not I?" Think instead, "Oh, I will look upon his success much as I would if it was my younger brother who earned all that money. His success is my success." This quality is termed *maitri* or friendliness.

The next attitude is called *karuṇā*, or compassion. When you see people struggling or making mistakes, you should not develop an attitude of superiority: "I am greater than they. I have done so much. These people have not worked hard or they are at a low level." Rather, you should develop the compassionate insight that you also were in a similar situation in the process of your own evolution and probably even worse; yet you have evolved. Similarly, all these people are in the process of evolution. Further, who are you to judge them? It may seem to you that certain people are inferior to you, but in God's eye they may be superior. So, keep your judgment to yourself, control yourself, and have compassion.

When you come in contact with people who are highly advanced like sages and saints, you should feel a sense of joy that since such persons have accomplished the goal of Self-realization, you too can do the same. All great personages confirm your potentiality. This is called *mudita*, a spirit of joyousness toward superiors.

When you come into contact with people who are gross or degraded, you should treat them with indifference. Do not react to them at all. If such a degraded person were to come up to you and call you a "donkey," do not argue with him or try to convince him that you could not be a donkey! There is no need to say even one word. Just remain unmoved, as if he were talking to a wall.

If you adopt these attitudes, handle your mind externally

as well as internally, and have God-realization as the goal, then you are truly utilizing the gift of mind, and you are effectively thanking God for that gift. Even if you have attained a small degree of mental integration, that is a tremendous achievement. Gradually, you will be led to the unimaginable heights of spiritual attainment.

IV

The Greatest Friend

by Swami Chidananda

More precious than gold or silver or diamonds, more precious than any wealth, your greatest wealth, greatest asset, greatest power, greatest friend, and greatest helper is your mind. In your mind you have an ally. In your mind you have an ever-ready friend, twenty-four hours of the day and night. Even when you are alone, abandoned, helpless, or you are in dire distress, or in a dangerous predicament, your mind is there to help you ever ready at hand, to guide you, and to show you ways and means to overcome any situation.

Do not underestimate the value of your mind. It is your precious friend. It is your great well-wisher. It is an invaluable helper. It is a source of all good. Know it as such, treat it as such, utilize it as such. Then you will be wise. Then you will rejoice.

It is not always right to denigrate the mind, to think of it as your enemy. You can make it your enemy, or you can make it your greatest liability. If you are foolish, if you are thoughtless, if you are not wise, if you have failed to grasp this important implication of the scriptures and the teachings of great teachers, then you will always be struggling with your mind. You will be lamenting in your mind, "I want to be very good, but my mind is very bad to me. It is not allowing me to do good. I am really a good person, but my mind is dragging me down. Mind is doing this, mind is doing that."

It is not so. On the contrary, you do not give your mind a

chance, you are very unkind to your mind. You do not recognize its precious value, you have not understood it. You are doing what is called, "Give a dog a bad name and then hang it." You are committing sins of commission, and an even greater number of sins of omission, toward the mind. Mind is *parā śakti*, mind is God's gift to the individual soul, mind can grant you liberation. There is nothing in the whole world that is so constantly at your beck and call, so constantly ever ready, ever present to do your bidding and to help.

Safeguarding the Mind

The whole career of a surgeon may depend upon the condition of his surgical instruments. The whole career of a master painter is in his brushes and his colors. The life of a soldier depends upon the condition of his rifle. Have you considered how carefully they look after and care for that upon which their entire life depends, their entire career depends? Dancers will insure their legs for millions of dollars; master pianists will insure each finger for millions of dollars. They care for and guard carefully that which they depend upon, and it, in turn, is good to them, helps them, gives them everything they want.

Therefore, you should also safeguard your mind, protect it, take great care of it, and treat it with kindness. Its enemies are *rajo guṇa* (passion) and *tamo guṇa* (laziness). Its enemies are temptation in the form of outer attractions, the inveterate habitual tendencies of the senses toward sense objects. Its enemies lie in the lower self—lust, anger, and greed.

Guard your mind from the lower self, from these dark, negative tendencies, from bad company, from idleness and from the assailment of old *saṁskāras* (mental impressions). Keep it occupied, keep it positive, take it into good company. Try to keep it in an elevated state. Do not allow the lower mind to drag it down. Be your own best friend. Be the best friend of your mind; befriend it.

Then, what will it not do for you? There is nothing that it will not do for you; it will do everything that you want. It depends upon your way of dealing with it, your recognition of its preciousness, its true place in your life, its great significance and its meaning for your liberation, for your highest good. Be good to your mind. Do justice to it. Do not always throw stones, or make it a scapegoat. Realize that it is God who has given you your mind, and therefore you are a human being; otherwise you would be an animal. And when God has made you a person with a mind, be a real human being.

Think deeply. Then you will realize what the mind is to you. It is to be utilized, channeled, it is to be educated, strengthened, and supported in every way. You must nurture it and make it your greatest asset. This requires clear perception, wisdom, and active effort. It is laziness that ruins the mind. Take pains, be willing to take the trouble. You will not regret it. It will repay you a thousandfold. Ponder well this inner situation of yours. Ponder well this fact: how great a thing the mind is, how much you owe it.

V

Seeking Comfort Within

by Swami Satchidananda

What you think, you ultimately become. If you think that you are a negative person, you do not need any other negativity coming from anywhere else to make that true—you are making yourself negative.

When this happens, you have to analyze it. "Are these thoughts good for me? Is it helpful for me to have these thoughts? Is it constructive or destructive? If my thoughts are negative, what will I become?" When you realize the negative effect you will not even want to think that way anymore.

People do not think seriously about the effect that thoughts have on them. Even if you are not negative about yourself, if you have negative thoughts about others, it will affect *you* negatively. If you hate somebody, you are ruining your life by your hatred. It is not only charity that begins at home. Even hatred begins at home. People who hate others will be filled with hatred themselves. If you are angry with another person, before your anger affects that person, it will have affected you. For example, think of a gun and imagine shooting at a target. Before the bullet goes out and hits the target, it has heated up the barrel. So the gun itself became affected first. In a way there is a backfire. Likewise every thought that comes from your mind—even before it leaves the mind—can ruin or improve you.

So, at least for your own sake, if not for the sake of others, you should not develop any negative thoughts about yourself or about anybody else. Anyone who is interested in his or her own welfare—physical and mental—should not invite negative thoughts.

Self-Love

Question: How does one find self-love?

Sri Gurudev: Love yourself. Think, "I am God's child. God has given me all these gifts. I love myself because God is functioning through me."

Even if you have some problems, you should still not think that God does not love you. That is where we see karma at work. You must have done something before and now the result has come. "God is merciful, so He is purging my karma by having me go through this." Just as a doctor has to operate in certain cases, so God operates on us when necessary. In the case of the doctor, we at least know exactly what happened. But with karma, we have probably forgotten. Still, there must be a cause because nothing happens without a cause. So when you think of all these things, remember: "Yes, God loves me. I am the dear, dear child of God." Think of all the gifts that God has given and you will learn to love God. By loving God you will also love yourself.

Self-Judgment

Question: Sri Gurudev how do we stop self-judgment?

Sri Gurudev: Why should we stop self-judgment? You have to judge yourself. You need to analyze and think, "How am I doing? Am I doing right or wrong? How is my mind? Is it selfish or not?" There is nothing wrong in this kind of self-judgment or self-analysis. We need to do it.

It is better to judge yourself than to judge others. You should not judge others without first judging yourself. You have to make sure that you are a good judge. Who will be a good judge?

Will it be the one who is the relative of the plaintiff or the close friend of the defendant? No, it will be the neutral person. That is why in many courts, over the head of the judge, hangs the picture of justice, a balance. That means a judge is a yogi, a neutral person. Such a person should judge himself or herself. "Am I neutral? Or am I leaning to this side or that side?" If you are already leaning to one side, you have no right to judge anybody else because you are not on the neutral level. A balance that is not in the neutral position cannot give the correct weight. You have to bring it to zero first to get the exact weight.

Every morning you stand on a scale in the bathroom. If the pointer is not on zero can you get the right weight? Can you judge your weight correctly? No. You have to set it to zero. In the same way, your mind should be set at zero, not leaning this way or that way. You cannot be prejudiced. That is a good judge. So you have every right to judge yourself and see if you are maintaining yourself in the neutral position. Until that time do not try to judge anybody else because your judgment will be wrong.

Turning to God

Question: Why do we want so much to be loved? Why are we not content just to love others? Why do we fear rejection? Why do we crave emotional comfort? Why do we want others to care about us?

Sri Gurudev: We want these things when we still have not realized that there is always Somebody in us who is caring for and loving us every minute. If only you realized that you would not need somebody else to love you. The more you look for somebody else to love you, the more difficult it will be to get that love.

Even rejection is a helpful thing because ultimately, it will make you turn inward and say, "Nobody seems to be loving me. God, You are the only one to love me." If others love you, you may forget God also, saying, "God I am happy with that person.

I do not need to worry about You now." But when everything fails, you turn to God.

God really loves you and that seems to be the very reason why He (or She) does not want you to go looking for love from anywhere else. He is helping you to turn totally toward Him. If we feel that presence in us why do we need any other comfort? The best Comforter is inside. All other kinds of comfort are temporary, they will come and go. Outside things and people are not always going to make you happy. It is that way so that one day you will know that there is always Something inside.

If the world could make people happy, there would not be any churches, synagogues, or spiritual centers. Nobody would read the holy scriptures. Why? Because the money and the friends made you happy. Why would you need anything else then? So to turn to God, all other things should make you unhappy.

I am sorry, it is a little hard-hearted to say this. But everything must deceive you ultimately and hit you so hard that you turn back to God. That is what will happen to a sincere seeker. That is God's will.

God says to us, "You want to trust Me totally. If you do that, I will give you everything, eternal happiness. Why go running after little things when I can give you everything?" If God cannot stop you from running after everything, He allows you to go learn for yourself. "Okay, go, get hit. Then come back to Me." Until that is felt inside, this kind of disappointment will keep happening, and the more it happens the happier you should be. "Ah, yes, God is helping me to turn within soon."

When people are not ready to realize God, they will be tempted to go out searching for happiness and they will be given piecemeal happiness here and there. When people find a lot of pleasure outside in the world, it shows that God is not in a hurry to get them. If God is in a hurry to get you, He will make you displeased with everything outside very soon. That is why in the life histories of all the saints, the minute they become conscious of God, they got into all kinds of problems, all kinds of troubles. Suffering after suffering came to them. Why? God said, "Ah, you really want Me; you should come quickly to Me. I will make everybody and everything hit you fast so that you can come to Me soon."

Imagine that I have a dog who always runs away and goes into the neighbor's houses. What should I do? I can say to the neighbors, "Any time my dog comes into your house, hit him." If the neighbors do that, where will the dog go? Back to me. On the other hand if they give him nice treats and cookies, the dog will be tempted to leave my house and go there again and again.

That is exactly what has happened with God. He has told all the neighbors (the worldly things), "Hit her, hit him. Let this child come back to Me soon. Do not tempt this one with your cookies." That is the proof that God is interested in getting you all for Himself.

PART TWO

Using the Gift Wisely

Seek ye first the good things of the mind,
and the rest will either be supplied
or its loss will not be felt.

Francis Bacon

Ordinary minds are scattered all over the world. We try to capture and possess everything that we see, like a giant octopus. Whenever water falls from a high mountain onto a rock it scatters all over into small sprays and drops and does not flow anymore. Similarly, our thoughts have fallen on the hard rock of self-consciousness and are scattered all over the world. Therefore, we cannot collect them.

When water falls upon another mass of water, however, it merges into a constant flow. It is no longer scattered, but it mixes in with that water. If our mind, instead of falling on self-consciousness, goes toward the ocean of Divine Unity then it will no longer be scattered, it will be unified. It will flow into the ocean and become part of it. That would be the state when we realize the oneness between ourselves and divinity.

Swami Abhedananda
Mystery of Death

VI

Freeing the Mind

by Ram Dass and Stephen Levine

How do you use your thoughts and how do you transcend them? And how do you go beyond mind? When you acknowledge that your life is a vehicle for your liberation it becomes clear that all of your life experiences are the optimum experience you need in order to awaken. And the minute you perceive them that way they are useful within that domain. The minute you ignore that perception, they will not work that way.

In psychology there is a term called "functional fixedness." It is like when you look at a hammer and you think of a hammer as an instrument to hammer nails. You might need something to serve as a pendulum but every time you look at the hammer you only see something to hammer nails. The idea that the hammer could be attached to a string and used as a pendulum does not come through because the ego cannot break the functional fixedness; you have got a set mind about how it is supposed to be and you cannot break that set.

Well, it is the same thing with life experiences. A culture has a set about what the meaning of experiences are all about. Like what death is about or what deviant behavior is about. Is it insanity, or is it mystical wisdom? There are all these models in a culture, all its functional fixedness that you absorb as to what your life experiences are about. Is it gratifying, is it pleasant or painful? The model this culture works within is a model of gratification through external agents, getting more from the environment, man over nature, control and mastery for gratification, for creating your own personal heaven in which your ego stays paramount, your ego is "God." And that is different from a culture such as the Hopi Indians where you hear about a balance of man and nature, harmony, the Tao, the flow. Man *in* nature rather than man *over* nature. It is not mastery and control; it is listening to hear the way in which you play a part in the flow. Then it is not just your personal gratification; it is you being part of a process that transcends your own separateness. That is a way of talking about God, that is God in form.

So the models you have of your experiences in your mind determine whether that experience can liberate you or will continue to entrap you. This is the beginning of the use of the mind. This is discriminative awareness. That is, making the discrimination between those things, or those ways of looking at things, that will bring you close to God, to your own freedom; and those things which take you away from it.

Now at the stage that many people I meet are at they do their practice, their method, as "good" and as well as they can. And then they take a little time off. They say, "Well that has been great; now what do you say we have a pizza and a beer and listen to some good music." Now that—pizza, beer, and music—could do it for them too except in their mind there is a model that the "time off" has nothing to do with it. We have got these models in our head about what is going to get us there. Meditation we suppose will get us there, pizza we presume will not. But the pizza, beer, and rock music could do it for you if you were open to the flow of it, but the meditation might not if you are busy being righteous about it. There is no act in and of itself that is either *dharmic* or *adharmic*. It is who is doing it and why they are doing it that determines whether it is wholesome or not. To stick a knife in somebody can be *adharmic*, taking people away from God, or if you are a surgeon it could be bringing them to God. Obviously the act of the knife into the person is not the issue. It is who is doing what, how. Even two surgeons could use that knife differently, one *dharmically*, the other *adharmically*; yet both think they are trying to save somebody. One is tuned to God's will and one is not. One is on an ego trip of "I will save you," and one is healing in the way of things, and says, "If it be Thy will, O Lord."

The statement, "If it be Thy will, O Lord," is "If it be in the nature of things, if it be in the Natural Law, if it be in the flow of perfection of form." God, or the Natural Law, or the Divine Law, does not have to be judged by you. It has to be understood by you and heard by you and felt by you, and *be'd* by you.

Keeping the Goal in View

So you ask yourself, "How do I use my every moment to get there?" Not heavy, tight, "I have got to be careful, I might make a mistake." Light, dancing, trusting, quieting, flowing. It has got to be done with the flow of love and the quietness of mind. It is like the women in India who go to the well and come back with a jug full of water on their heads. They are talking and gossiping as they walk, but they never forget the jug of water on their head. The jug of water is what your journey is all about. In the course of it you do what you do in life, but you do not forget the jug of water. You do not forget what it is all about. You keep your eye on the mark. At first you have to prime the pump a little bit to do it; and you keep forgetting and remembering and forgetting and remembering. That is what the illusion is. The illusion keeps pulling you back into forgetting. Lost in your melodrama: my love life, my child, my livelihood, my gratification. "Somebody ripped off my stereo," "I do not have a thing to wear," . . . just more and more stuff. And you keep forgetting it.

And then every now and then you remember. You sit down and meditate or you read Ramakrishna or Ramana Maharshi and suddenly, "Oh, yeah right; whew! That is what it was about." And you remember again. And then a moment later you forget.

But what happens is the balance shifts. If you can imagine a wheel whose rim is the cycle of births, all of the stuff of life, conditioned reality, and whose center is perfect flow, formless no-mind, the source. You have got one foot with most of your weight on the circumference of the wheel, and one foot tentatively on the center. That is the beginning of awakening. And you come in and you sit down and meditate and suddenly there is a moment when you feel the perfection of your being and your connection. And even beyond that, you just are. You are just like a tree or a stream. There is only a second or two of it there at the hub. Then your weight goes back on the outside of the wheel. Over and over and over this happens. Slowly, slowly the weight shifts. Then the weight shifts just enough so that there is a slight predominance on the center of the wheel, and you find that you naturally just want to sit down and be quiet. You do not have to say, "I have got to meditate now." Or, "I have got to read a holy book." Or, "I have got to turn off the television set." Or, I have got to do anything. It does not become that kind of a discipline any more. The balance has shifted. And you keep allowing your life to become more and more simple. More and more harmonious. And less and less are you grabbing at this and pushing that away.

You are listening to hear how it is rather than imposing a structure because you see that if you keep imposing structure it does not get you freer. And you begin to forget your own romantic story-line. "Who am I becoming?" "What will I be when I grow up?" All of these models just fall away. You just start to sit simply, live simply, be where you are, be with who you are with when you are with them; you hear your *dharma*. If it is making shoes, you make shoes. And you are making the shoe with your consciousness in the present, simple and easy, not having a fantasy of surfing in Hawaii. You are just making a shoe. And because of the consciousness that you are bringing into that making of a shoe, the no-mind quality of it, it becomes the perfect statement of *shoe-ness* that can come through you in view of your skills at that moment.

When you can just make a shoe while you make a shoe you *are* the meditation. There is nothing to do. Your whole life is a meditative act. There is no time you leave meditation. It is not just sitting on your meditation pillow, your zafu. All of life is a big zafu; no matter whether you are driving or making love or whatever you are doing. It is all meditation. It becomes interesting to reflect on your life as to which acts can be done from the zafu and which cannot. Which acts would fall away were they done from this space of just clear quiet presence? It is just a natural shedding that occurs as part of the process which we are all in. . . .

Discriminative Awareness

A skillful use of the intellect is contemplation. Every morning work with a thought. Take a holy book. Do not read pages, do not collect it; take one thought and just sit with it for about ten or fifteen minutes.

You could contemplate on the qualities of Christ. Charity. Suffering. Every day you contemplate on the stuff you are becoming. Sri Ramakrishna said, "If you meditate on your ideal, you will acquire its nature. If you think of God day and night, you will acquire the nature of God."

Fill your mind with things that are going to get you there. Your mind does not have to be filled with the daily news to prove that you are a good citizen. You do not have to be at the mercy of all this, the constant onslaught of media. You could fill your mind instead with the stuff that liberates you. Ultimately becoming aware of that which gets you to God and that which does not, to help you let go of that which does not.

You begin to develop the power of your mind through concentration, through one-pointedness. Following the breath, following the mantra, whatever is your *dharmic* choice. You develop the capacity to put your mind on one thought and keep it there and let everything else flow by. You do not stop your mind. You let it flow. But you bring one thought constantly to the surface. You keep coming back to one thought all the time. Breathing in, breathing out, breathing in, breathing out. Rising, falling. You note breathing in, or you use your mantra, "Ram, Ram, Ram, Ram." Eating, sleeping, . . . "Ram, Ram." You "Ram-ize" it. You convert it all by maintaining a frame of reference. That has the dual capacity of centering you and increasing the power of one-pointedness. A one-pointed mind is free of the intellect, it is a supple, useful mind.

You see, you can use your intellect to judge the universe or to clean up your own game. If you judge the universe, you are using your intellect to take you away from God; if you use it to clean up your own game, it can take you toward God, toward the Tao, the way of things, the Divine Plan as discussed in Judaism, Christianity, the Moslem religion, Hinduism, Zoroastrianism; you could call it the Mind of God, you could call it the Natural Law, you could call it the way in which everything in form is related to everything else. That is the flow; and that flow is harmonious in its parts. Even the cacophonous parts are harmonious, in the larger scope of things. They are not lawful in linear, analytic, logical sense. Natural Law includes paradox, which logical law cannot.

"A" can be "A" and "not-A" at the same moment. It is not a law that you know with your intellect. It is a law that you can become, but you cannot know. The closest we come to a sensing of the law is what we call intuitive wisdom in the West. Gurdjieff called it "the higher faculty." It is a higher way of knowing, a subjective involvement in the universe; not an objective one. You do not know the law; you are the law. And you sense, when you have a quiet mind, the way of things.

Just as some American Indian tribes would send a pubescent boy out into the wilderness for a few days or weeks to fast and listen, to become quiet, and attune to the way of things; so it is necessary to get quiet enough to hear, not only the singing mating calls of the birds, but the way of your own sexual desires, the way of your own patterns of anger, the way of your own heart, the way of the decay of your own body, without getting lost in grabbing hold, in judgment or analysis or clinging or fear; but just hearing it as it is. It is not the objective "witness" in the sense of standing back and looking. It is a subjective being part of it without attachment anywhere. It is a very subtle place I am talking about now. It is the use of the mind beyond the intellect. The intellect is the first step of it, discriminative awareness; looking around and saying, "This anger is not going to get me to God, I am going to drop it." You drop it because you see where you are going this lifetime. It is like going to New York City and you come to a road which leads to Mexico, but you do not take it this time. Mexico is beautiful but it is not where you are going this time around.

Discriminative awareness is based on goal-oriented behavior. But as you get near the end of the journey, you must give up even the concepts of the goal, and of the trying, and of you being someone seeking. Because even those concepts ultimately keep you back. All concepts, all models, all molds, all programs in your head, are limiting conditions. No-mind, the sufficient faith to exist in no-mind, to just be empty and trust that as a situation arises, out of you will come what is necessary to deal with that situation including the use of your intellect where appropriate. Your intellect need not be constantly held on to, to keep reassuring you that you know where you are at, out of fear of loss of control. Ultimately, when you stop identifying so much with your physical body and with your psychological entity, that anxiety starts to disintegrate. And you start to define yourself as in flow with the universe; and whatever comes along—death, life, joy, sadness—is grist for the mill of awakening. Not "this" versus "that," but "whatever."

VII

Building Character

by Yogi Ramacharaka

The molding, modifying, changing, and building of character is largely a matter of the establishing of habits. And our next question becomes, "What is the best way to establish habits?" The answer of the Yogi is: "Establish a mental image, and then build your habit around it." And in that sentence he has condensed a whole system.

Everything that has a form is built around a mental image—either the mental image of some person, some animal, or of the Absolute. This is the rule of the universe, and in the matter of character-building we but follow a well-established rule. When we wish to build a house, we first think of "house" in a general way. Then we begin to think of what kind of house. Then we go into details. We consult an architect, and he makes us a plan, which is his mental image, suggested by our mental image. Once the plan has been decided upon we consult the builder, and at last the house stands completed—an objectified mental image. And so it is with every created thing—all manifestations of a mental image.

Therefore, when we wish to establish a character trait, we must form a clear, distinct mental image of what we wish to be. This is an important step. Make your picture clear and distinct, and fasten it in your mind. Then begin to build around it. Let your thoughts dwell upon the mental picture. Let your imagination see yourself as possessed of the desired trait, and acting it out. Act it out in your imagination, over and over again, as often as possible, persevering, and continuously seeing yourself manifesting the trait under a variety of circumstances and conditions. As you continue to do this you will find that you will gradually begin to express the thought in action—to objectify the subjective mental image. It will become natural for you to act more and more in accordance with your mental image, until at last the new habit will become firmly fixed in your mind, and will become your natural mode of action and expression.

This is no vague, visionary theory. It is a well known and proven psychological fact, and thousands have worked marvelous changes in their character by its means.

Not only may one elevate one's moral character in this way, but he may mold his "workaday" self to better conform to the needs of his environment and occupation. If one lacks perseverance, he may attain it; if one is filled with fear, he may supplant it with fearlessness; if one lacks self-confidence, he may gain that. In fact, there is no trait that may not be developed in this way. People have literally "made themselves over" by following this method of character-building. The great trouble with the race has been that people have not realized that they could do these things. They have thought that they were doomed to remain just the creatures that they found themselves to be. They did not realize that the work of creation was not ended, and that they had within themselves a creative power adapted to the needs of their case. When man first realizes this truth, and proves it by practice, he becomes another being. He finds himself superior to his environment and training—he finds that he may ride over these things. He makes his own environment, and he trains himself. . . .

We cannot attempt, in the short space of a single lesson, to map out a course of instruction in character-building adapted to the special needs of each individual. But we think that what we have said on the subject should be sufficient to point out the method for each student to map out a course for himself, following the general rules given above. As a help to the student, however, we will give a brief course of instruction for the cultivation of one desirable trait of character. The general plan of this course may be adapted to fit the requirements of any other case, if intelligence is used by the student. The case we have selected is that of a student who has been suffering from: A lack of moral courage, a lack of self-confidence, an inability to maintain any poise in the presence of other people, an inability to say 'No,' a feeling of inferiority with those with whom one comes in contact. A brief outline of the course of practice given in this case is herewith given.

Equality of Man

You should fix firmly in your mind the fact that you are the equal of any and every person. You come from the same source. You are an expression of the same one Life. In the eyes of the Absolute you are the equal of any person, even the highest in the land. . . . All feelings of inferiority are illusions, errors, and lies, and have no existence in Truth. When in the company of others remember this fact and realize that the Life Principle in you is talking to the Life Principle in them. Let the Life Principle flow through you, and endeavor to forget your personal self. At the same time, endeavor to see that same Life Principle, behind and beyond the personality of the person in whose presence you are. He is by a personality hiding the Life Principle, just as you are. Nothing more—nothing less! You are both one in Truth.

Let the consciousness of the "I" beam forth and you will experience an uplift and sense of courage, and the other will likewise feel it. You have within you the Source of courage, moral and physical, and you have naught to fear—fearlessness is your Divine Heritage, avail yourself of it. You have self-confidence, for the Self is the "I" within you, not the petty personality, and you must have confidence in that "I." Retreat within yourself until you feel the presence of the "I," and then you will have a self-confidence that nothing can shake or disturb. Once having attained the permanent consciousness of the "I," you will have poise. Having realized that you are a center of power, you will have no difficulty to say no when it is right to do so. Once having realized your true nature—your real Self—you will lose all sense of inferiority, and will know that you are a manifestation of the one Life and have behind you the strength, power, and grandeur of the cosmos. Begin by realizing your Self, and then proceed with the following methods of training the mind.

Positive Attitude

It is difficult for the mind to build itself around an idea, unless that idea can be expressed in words. A word is the center of an idea, just as the idea is the center of the mental image, and the mental image the center of the growing mental habit. Therefore, the yogis always lay great stress upon the use of words in this way. In the particular case before us we should suggest the holding before you of a few words crystallizing the main thought.

We suggest the words "I am," "courage," "confidence," "poise," "firmness," "equality." Commit these words to memory, and then endeavor to fix in your mind a clear conception of the meaning of each word, so that each may stand for a live idea when you say it. Beware of parrot-like or phonographic repetition. Let each word's meaning stand out clearly before you, so that when you repeat it you may feel its meaning. Repeat the words frequently when an opportunity presents itself, and you will soon begin to notice that they act as a strong mental tonic upon you, producing a bracing, energizing effect. Each time you repeat the words, understandingly, you have done something to clear away the mental path over which you wish to travel.

Applications

When you are at leisure, and are able to indulge in

daydreams without injury to your affairs of life, call your imagination into play and endeavor to picture yourself as being possessed of the qualities indicated by the words named. Picture yourself under the most trying circumstances, making use of the desired qualities, and manifesting them fully. Endeavor to picture yourself as acting out your part well and exhibiting the desired qualities. Do not be ashamed to indulge in these daydreams, for they are the prophecies of the things to follow, and you are but rehearsing your part before the day of the performance. Practice makes perfect, and if you accustom yourself to acting in a certain way in imagination, you will find it much easier to play your part when the real performance occurs. This may seem childish to many of you, but if you have an actor among your acquaintances, consult him about it, and you will find that he will heartily recommend it. He will tell you what practice does for one in this direction, and how repeated practice and rehearsals may fix a character so firmly in a person's mind that he may find it difficult to divest himself of it after a time. Choose well the part you wish to play—the character you wish to be—and then after fixing it well in your mind, practice, practice, and practice. Keep your ideal constantly before you, and endeavor to grow into it. And you will succeed, if you exercise patience and perseverance.

More than this, do not confine your practice to mere private rehearsal. You need some "dress rehearsals" as well—rehearsals in public. Therefore, after you get well started in your work, exercise your growing character-habits in your everyday life. Pick out the little cases first and try it on them. You will find that you will be able to overcome conditions that formerly bothered you. You will become conscious of a growing strength and power coming from within, and you will recognize that you are indeed a changed person. Let your thought express itself in action, whenever you get a chance. But do not try to force chances just to try your strength. Do not, for instance, try to force people to ask for favors so that they may have to refuse. You will find plenty of genuine tests without forcing any. Accustom yourself to looking people in the eye, and feeling the power that is behind you and within you. You will soon be able to see through their personality, and realize that it is just one portion of the one Life gazing at another portion, and that therefore there is nothing to be afraid of. A realization of your real Self will enable you to maintain your poise under trying circumstances, if you will but throw aside your false idea about your personality. Forget yourself—your little personal self—for a while, and fix your mind on the universal Self of which you are a part. All these things that have worried you, are but incidents of the personal life, and are seen to be illusions when viewed from the standpoint of the universal Life.

Carry the universal Life with you as much as possible into your everyday life. It belongs there as much as anywhere, and will prove to be a tower of strength and refuge to you in the perplexing situations of your busy life.

Remember always that the ego is master of the mental states and habits, and that the will is the direct instrument of the ego, and is always ready for its use. Let your soul be filled with the strong desire to cultivate those mental habits that will make you strong. Nature's plan is to produce strong individual expressions of herself, and she will be glad to give you her aid in becoming strong. The person who wishes to strengthen himself will always find great forces backing him to aid him in the work, for is he not carrying out one of nature's pet plans, and one which she has been striving for throughout the ages? Anything that tends to make you realize and express your mastery, tends to strengthen you, and places at your disposal nature's aid. You may witness this in everyday life—nature seems to like strong individuals, and delights in pushing them ahead. By mastery, we mean mastery over your own lower nature, as well as over outside nature, of course. The "I" is Master—forget it not, O student, and assert it constantly.

VIII

The Virtue
of Tolerance

by Luella Cole

Most people seem to have a secret yen to make over their friends, acquaintances, and relatives into a model that would suit them better. Sometimes the proposed revisions of personality would be for the best, but this fact does not make them any more likely of success. One of the harder things about accepting reality is the realization that people are what they are and that it is easier to adapt yourself to them than to adapt them to you. Not that children cannot be educated out of many faults, or that adults cannot reeducate themselves. It is, however, a rare adult who can be altered by anyone but himself.

For instance, my grandfather got completely rid of his irascible temper. Sternly curing himself after he had one day hurled a hammer across the room in exasperation, only to have it connect with his wife's forehead as she entered the room and knock her out for several hours. He never lost his temper again, but the reform came from within; his parents, teachers, friends, and even his wife had been trying in vain to cure him for years. Although self-reformation sometimes occurs when the motive is strong enough, people do not usually alter greatly as they grow older. They are what God and their experiences to date have made them, and there is not much that another person can do about it, once they have reached adult years.

Anyone who can accept humanity as it is has made a great step forward in facing reality as an adult. A truly mature person can resist the temptation to reform others except indirectly through his own example and can concentrate upon reforming himself. What I regard as a mature attitude was expressed by an acquaintance when she said that she did not tinker with her friends' personalities because she liked them the way they were—faults and all—because she thought their traits none of her business, and because a program of reformation would bore her to death. I would add a further and very practical reason: that one is almost sure to lose his friends if he tries to glue on a trait here and lop another off there.

Overcoming Hero-Worship

It is inevitable that an intelligent person will see faults in those to whom he or she is most attached. Only a young person who is tremendously in love or a child who is uncritical can regard another person as one hundred percent perfect. Sane people see the faults in others but they simply do not care. It is my own opinion that if another person's virtues outweigh his faults, one has no business asking for more.

Immature adults may take refuge in the prolongation of childish credulity or adolescent hero-worship. As a little girl a woman may have adored her mother; as an adolescent, one of her teachers; and as an adult, her husband. In each case she sees perfection in the object of her devotion. Such a woman has not matured emotionally and she is ill prepared for the inevitable discovery that her love will not automatically confer sainthood upon those she adores. Other adults have one attack of hero-worship after another throughout their adolescent years and then fall in love upon the same basis. As a means of education hero-worship is excellent if a worthy hero is chosen, because the worshiper strives to copy his model, but as a fundamental pattern of adult life it is inadequate. Sooner or later the feet of clay come into view, and the more abject the worship, the greater the shock at their appearance. The adult has to learn that even the dearest of loved ones is as full of human frailty as any other individual. As a first reaction to this knowledge, the immature person may become cynical and sardonic because he cannot accept the revelation of reality. This attitude is as childish as either blind devotion or unquestioning hero-worship. It is merely negative instead of positive. No matter how cleverly or with what refinements of sophistication it may be expressed, it is still childish.

Accepting people as they are, loving them, faults and all, refusing to give unasked-for-advice, showing a great tolerance of humanity and its foibles, admitting an equal right to exist to those who do not especially appeal to you, and being willing to make such adaptations as you can to the personality of others— these are to my mind the attitudes of grown-up people. Such attitudes do not prevent love. Quite the contrary! They permit love to be based upon truth instead of upon illusion.

IX

The Systematic Development of Mind

by Swami Vivekananda

The main difference between human beings and animals is the difference in their power of concentration. All success in any line of work is the result of this. Everybody knows something about concentration. We see its results every day. High achievements in art, music, and so on are the result of concentration. An animal has very little power of concentration. Those who have trained animals find much difficulty in the fact that the animal is constantly forgetting what is told to him. He cannot concentrate his mind upon anything for long. Therein lies the difference between a human being and an animal—a human being has greater power of concentration. Differences in their power of concentration also constitutes the difference between people. Compare the lowest with the highest person. The difference is in the degree of concentration. This is the only difference.

Everybody's mind becomes concentrated at times. We all concentrate upon those things we love, and we love those things upon which we concentrate our minds. What mother is there that does not love the face of her homeliest child? That face is to her the most beautiful in the world. She loves it because she concentrates her mind on it; and if everyone could concentrate his mind on that same face, everyone would love it. It would become the most beautiful face to all. When we hear beautiful music, our minds become fastened upon it and we cannot take them away. Those who concentrate their minds upon what you call classical music do not like popular music, and vice versa. Music in which the notes follow each other in rapid succession holds the mind readily. A child loves lively music because the rapidity of the notes gives the mind no chance to wander. One who likes popular music generally dislikes classical music, because it is more complicated and requires a greater degree of concentration.

The great trouble with such concentration is that we do not control the mind; it controls us. Something outside of ourselves, as it were, draws the mind into it and holds it as long as it chooses. We hear melodious tones or see a beautiful painting, and the mind is held fast, we cannot take it away.

If I speak well on a subject you like, your mind becomes concentrated upon what I am saying. I draw your mind away from yourself and hold it upon the subject in spite of yourself. Thus, our attention is held, our minds are concentrated upon various things, in spite of ourselves. We cannot help it.

The Power of Detachment

Now the question is: can this concentration be developed, and can we become masters of it? The yogis say yes. The yogis say that we can get perfect control of the mind. On the ethical side there is danger in the development of the power of concentration—the danger of concentrating the mind upon an object and then being unable to detach it at will. This state causes great suffering. Almost all our suffering is caused by our not having the power of detachment. Therefore, along with the development of concentration we must also develop the power of detachment. We must learn not only to attach the mind to one thing exclusively, but also to detach it at a moment's notice and place it upon something else. These should be developed together to make it safe.

This is the systematic development of the mind. To me, the very essence of education is concentration of mind, not the collecting of facts. If I had to do my education over again, and had any voice in the matter, I would not study facts at all. I would develop the power of concentration and detachment, and then with a perfect instrument I could collect facts at will. Side by side, a child should be developing the power of concentration and detachment.

My development has been one-sided all along. I developed concentration without the power of detaching my mind at will, and the most intense suffering of my life has been due to this. Now I have the power of detachment, but I had to learn it later in life. We should put our minds on things; they should not draw our minds to them. We are usually forced to concentrate. Our minds are forced to become fixed upon different things by an attraction to them which we cannot resist. To control the mind, to place it just where we want it, requires special training. It cannot be done in any other way. In the study of religion the control of the mind is absolutely necessary. In this study we have to turn the mind back upon itself.

The Science of Breathing

In training the mind the first step is to begin with the breathing. Regular breathing puts the body in a harmonious condition; and it is then easier to reach the mind. In practicing breathing, the first thing to consider is *āsana* or posture. Any posture in which a person can sit easily is his proper position. The spine should be kept free, and the weight of the body should be supported by the ribs. The three parts of the body, the chest, the neck, and the head must always be held in one straight line. Do not try by contrivances to control the mind; simple breathing is all that is necessary in that line. All austerities to gain concentration of the mind are a mistake. Do not practice them.

The mind acts on the body, and the body in its turn acts upon the mind. They act and react upon each other. Every mental state creates a corresponding state in the body, and every action in the body has its corresponding effect on the mind. It makes no difference whether you think the body and mind are two different entities, or whether you think they are both but one body—the physical body being the gross part and the mind the finer part. They act and react upon each other. The mind is constantly becoming the body. In the training of the mind, it is easier to reach it through the body. The body is easier to grapple with than the mind.

The finer the instrument, the greater the power. The mind is much finer and more powerful than the body. For this reason it is easier to begin with the body.

The science of breathing is that of working through the body to reach the mind. In this way we get control of the body, and then we begin to feel the finer working of the body, the finer and more interior, and so on till we reach the mind. As we feel the finer workings of the body, they come under our control. After a while you will be able to feel the operation of the mind on the body. You will also feel the working of one half of the mind upon the other half, and also feel the mind recruiting the nerve centers; for the mind controls and governs the nervous system. You will feel the mind operating along the different nerve currents. Thus the mind is brought under control—by regular systematic breathing, by governing the gross body first and then the finer body.

X

Obstacles to Mental Liveliness

by Jules Z. Willing

If you listen carefully to what people say about their own mental ability, you will observe that most of it is disparaging. Within half an hour in my classroom, I heard an intelligent man say that he did not keep a journal because most of his thoughts were just "rubbish," a woman made a joke at her own expense by saying she "had a big tongue but a little mind," and another man told me that his mind was "always wandering" to things he would prefer not to think about, and that it was "too lazy" to concentrate on what he did want to think about. A woman asked me why I thought it was important for her to know what she was thinking, adding, "Most of what goes through my head is nonsense, or trivial."

I had long thought that this self-disparagement was a form of modesty, a kind of social convention, but I have concluded that it is not; in most cases it is a genuine appraisal. Many people really do deplore their minds, and the adjectives they use are the same they employ in referring to irresponsible children: lazy, undisciplined, wandering, idle.

The consequences are far more serious than one might suppose, for the mind reflects and responds to our own evaluation of it, and this opinion draws the boundaries of our mental universe; our mind will tend to be only as "good" as we think it is.

The way in which this works is both obvious and little noted. You will preserve and use only that portion of your own mental output that you think has some value. The only person

52

making judgments about the value of what is going through your mind is you. This is an enormous responsibility that most of us take very lightly; most of us do not think of it at all.

Consider this example. An obscure employee in the Swiss patent office—a young man in his twenties named Albert Einstein—had some thoughts about the nature of the universe. Fortunately, he considered them to be significant. Although he had never written a scientific paper, was not associated with any academic institution, did not move in scientific circles, and was ignorant of much of what had been published on the subject, he wrote not one but five papers, which he mailed to the editor of *Annals of Physics*. They lacked the usual references and citations, nor were they based on his own laboratory research or experiments. Unlike traditional scientific documents, they were simply statements about what he thought. They were ideas that eventually earned Einstein the Nobel prize and permanently changed our conceptions of time, space, gravity, electromagnetism, and the nature and shape of the universe.

We know this now, but Einstein could not have known that his ideas would have these tremendous consequences. The difference was that the young patent clerk decided his ideas had value. So he wrote them down and sent them in.

Consider what would have happened if, when these ideas passed through his mind, Einstein had considered them to be of interest to no one other than himself, or if he had thought that his ideas were interesting but not important. He would probably have thought about them a while and then gone on to other things. Like so many of the thoughts and ideas all of us have, they would have died in the silence of his mind.

This is a bad example, I admit. To use Einstein, who was a genius, as an illustration of the universal, is foolhardy. I do not mean to suggest that you might formulate ideas on the scale of the relativity theory (although I do not assume the contrary, either) or that only ideas of this significance have value. What I want to illustrate is that Einstein was the first and only person who made the judgment of the value of his own thoughts before deciding to communicate them to others. If that judgment had not been affirmative, we would never have heard of him.

Developing an Attentive Mind

Although we are the sole judges of what we think, we are by no means unbiased, fair, and impartial. Quite the opposite. More likely, we are critical of what we think, often harsh and disapproving, because we do not have a very high opinion of our minds. Theoretically, at least, any one of us is capable at any time of generating an idea that might shake the world. It can never cause the slightest tremor, however, until we first "pay attention to it," and then "decide it is worth expressing to someone else."

Every thought and idea that fails this two-part test passes into mental oblivion. It astonishes me that we take this responsibility so lightly.

Imagine you are alone in a permanently sealed room, completely cut off from the world. The only thing in the room other than yourself is a teleprinter, a machine that looks and acts like the ticker in a newspaper or stockbroker's office. It is the only link between you and the rest of the world. The machine ticks constantly, printing out information, ideas, messages. The endless roll of paper moves continuously, spilling from the machine to a wastebasket into which it falls. Tick-tick-tick. You can go over to it whenever you please, and read what it prints out. You can pull up the descending portion and read the last few bulletins, but if you keep pulling you will see that the paper dissolves as it enters the waste receptacle. Tick-tick-tick. Occasionally, a bell on the machine rings. You know this means something of urgency or importance is being printed. But for the most part, all you hear is the tick-tick-tick of the printer.

The machine is very much like your mind, which is always telling you something. It never stops talking to you. But you have the freedom to ignore it most of the time, if you choose.

You know that urgent messages—like "there is a car about to run you down"—will cause your bell to ring. All the other messages will remain available for a little while until they disappear into the wastebasket.

Every once in a while, you will look at what the ticker is printing. You might continue to watch for a while, but most of the time you will not pay much attention. Bulletins will be printed out, descend into the receptacle, and be gone without you ever reading them. You know there is always more where they came from. There is occasional repetition, but mostly there seems to be a continual new supply. Much of what it reports is of no special interest. You have other things to do. So you mostly rely on the bell to get your attention. Sometimes you wish the machine would stop ticking; it can become such a nuisance that you would like to shut it off. But it is your only link to the outside world, and you know that your life depends on it. So you tolerate it.

But what you are developing is the deadly habit of inattention. Although all the news of all the world—of your own private reality—is constantly pouring in to you, you ignore most of it.

The extent to which you pay attention to the printer is determined entirely by the importance you attach to messages from yourself. The invisible typist tick-tick-ticking into the machine is you. Whether you read the message or not.

It is important, then, to regard the mind with respect, because it makes us what we are. The unceasing act of creation taking place inside us is producing thoughts and ideas whose value is incalculable. But if we have already concluded that most of what we think is clutter and static, trivial and worthless, we will not examine our ideas carefully enough to find the value in them; we will ignore and discard them almost as fast as they appear.

But if we make an error when we fail to see the significance of one of our thoughts, there is no double-check, no other mind to say, "Wait a minute—take another look." For we are alone, entirely alone, in the privacy of our mind; there is no one but us to make the judgment of what is meaningful, what is worth saying or writing or acting on or thinking further about. And we will never know, can never know, how many times every day we do make such a mistake.

Overfamiliarity

Part of this under-appreciation of our own mental activity is due to our considering it commonplace—an incessant tick-tick-ticking we have heard all our lives. I suppose if you were a bird you would not consider it remarkable to be able to fly. "What is so special about flying?" you might chirp to another bird. "Don't we all do it?" A spider would likely consider spinning webs drudgery, a humdrum activity. It is we human beings, who cannot fly or spin webs, who marvel over the miracle of flight and the magic of webs.

Every human being has a mind capable of feats far more amazing than flying or web spinning. Yet, because each of us has a mind and each of us is constantly doing remarkable things with it, we do not consider this extraordinary. Does not everyone have a mind? Does not everyone think? What is so special about it?

Regaining the Sense of Wonder

We have lost sight of the wonder of the mind. Part of maintaining its liveliness is retaining or regaining that sense of wonder. It is not just that having a mind is wonderful; the fact that each mind is unique, original, different from every other in the world is even more wondrous.

You may reply, "Come on, now—I have respect for my mind, but when it comes to such things as awe and wonder, you may be going overboard. What does wonder have to do with it?"

Well, what are some things you might regard as wonderful? Computers? Robots? Space ships? Voyages to the rings of Saturn? Artificial life forms? Miracles of medical science? The Einstein theories? Electronic technology? Higher mathematics?

Poetry? All these are simply products of the human mind, which has a seemingly inexhaustible supply.

The mind is the only permanent frontier, the leading edge of our steadily arriving future. It is an unending act of creation. It has no analogy, no metaphor: it is the sole member of the class of things of which it is the only instance. It is alive, a product of its own operations, responsive to itself. There is no known limit to its capacity, of which we "use" only a very small part. Its potential is absolutely unlimited. It is the most highly developed life-form in the universe, already fully capable of stupendous things it has not yet begun to imagine. It is truly an awesome and wonderful thing.

We tend to think such rather grandiose descriptions apply to extraordinary and famous people or to some abstract and poetical concept of "mind," but not to us. We disregard the fact that each of us is extraordinary because each of us possesses a completely equipped mind of our own, and because there is no such thing as an ordinary mind. We tend too much to regard thinking as a rather commonplace feature of our inner existence.

A good deal of this disregard, this low opinion, is bred, it seems, by overfamiliarity. "If I am the one who is thinking it, it cannot be very important." As with the bird to whom flying is so familiar, "If I am able to do it, it cannot be so wonderful."

Overfamiliarity also breeds ignorance. If we do not appreciate our mind, we will be less attentive to what is going on inside it, and so we will never get to know it well. We expect it to go about its business and leave us alone; in return, we will pay it little attention except in emergencies.

In time, we start to lose the ready inner connection with which we were born, and find it harder to tune in to what our mind is doing, what we are thinking. If we are offered a penny for our thoughts, we are not able to express an authentic penny's worth (although we will fake it by inventing a thought to fill the order). Thus, we never fully develop our reflexive ability and often fail altogether to develop both the knowledge of our mind and skill in using it.

PART THREE

A Powerful Tool

*A thought becomes a word
and soon a deed.
Be careful of the thoughts.*

Swami Chinmayananda

There is enough power within you, if properly directed, to accomplish almost any reasonable aim. To energize that power you must harness it up with faith. You must have the will to believe, the courage to aspire, and the conviction that success is possible to any person who works for it intelligently and persistently.

J. C. Roberts

Develop such mental power that you can stand unshaken, no matter what comes, bravely facing anything in life. If you love God you should have faith and be prepared to endure when trials come. Don't be afraid of suffering. Keep your mind positive and strong. It is your inner experience that is most important.

Paramahansa Yogananda

XI

The Power of Thought

by Paramahansa Yogananda

We are what we *think* we are. The habitual inclination of our thoughts determines our talents and abilities, and our personality. Thus, some *think* they are writers or artists, industrious or lazy, and so on. What if you want to be other than what you presently think you are? You may argue that others have been born with the special talent you lack but want to have. This is true. But they had to cultivate the habit of that ability some time—if not in this life, then in a previous one. So whatever you want to be, start to develop that pattern now. You can instill any trend in your consciousness right now, provided you inject a strong thought in your mind; then your actions and whole being will obey that thought. Do not settle for a one-track mentality. You can succeed in any profession or do anything you put your mind to. Whenever others told me I would not be able to do something, I made up my mind that I could do it, and I did!

Few demonstrations of mind-power are more dramatic than the power of thought for good or ill on the health of the body. My Guru told me the following story: He had lost much weight because of a serious illness. During convalescence, he visited his Guru, Lahiri Mahasaya, who asked about his health. Sri Yukteswarji explained the cause of his delicate condition.

"So," Lahiri Mahasaya said, "you made yourself sick and now you think you are thin. But I am sure you will feel better tomorrow."

The next day, Gurudeva went exultantly to Lahiri Mahasaya and proclaimed, "Sir, with your blessings, I feel much better today."

Lahiri Mahasaya responded, "Your condition was indeed quite serious, and you are still frail. Who knows how you might feel tomorrow?"

The next day Sri Yukteswarji was again completely debilitated. He lamented to his Guru, "Sir, I am again ailing, I could hardly drag myself here to you."

Lahiri Mahasaya replied, "So once more you indispose yourself."

After some days of this alternating health and ill health, which followed exactly the expectation of Sri Yukteswarji's thoughts influenced by Lahiri Mahasaya's suggestions, my Guru realized the powerful lesson his teacher had been trying to teach him.

Lahiri Mahasaya said, "What is this? One day you say to me, 'I am well,' and the next day you say, 'I am sick.' It is not that I have been healing or indisposing you. It is your own thoughts that have made you alternately weak and strong."

Then Master said, "If I think I am well and that I have regained my former weight, will it be so?"

Lahiri Mahasaya answered, "It is so."

Guruji said, "At that very moment I felt both my strength and weight return. When I reached my mother's home that night, she was startled to see my changed condition and thought that I was swelling from dropsy. Many of my friends were so amazed at my sudden recovery that they became disciples of Lahiri Mahasaya."

Thought Creates Everything

Such phenomenal demonstrations are possible to those who possess the power of realization that everything is thought. When you have yet to attain that realization, you have to keep applying will and positive affirmation until you make thought work for you. *Thought is the matrix of all creation; thought created everything.* If you hold on to that truth with indomitable will, you can materialize any thought. There is nothing that can gainsay it. It was by that kind of powerful thought that Christ rebuilt his crucified body; and it is what he referred to when he said, "Therefore I say unto you, whatsoever things ye desire, when ye pray, believe that ye receive them, and ye shall receive them." (Mark II:24)

Once you have said, "I will," never give in. If you say, "I will never catch cold," and the next morning you have a terrible cold and are discouraged, you are allowing your will to remain weak. You must not get discouraged when you see something happening that is contrary to what you have affirmed. Keep on believing, knowing it will be so. If outwardly you say, "I will," but inwardly think, "I cannot," then you neutralize the power of thought and emasculate your will. If your will has become weakened by fighting disease or other reverses, you have to take the help of someone else's will to strengthen you through their prayers and positive affirmations on your behalf. But you must also do your part to change your consciousness. That is my advice to you. Develop your willpower and positive thinking, and you will find your body, mind, and soul working to mold everything in your life according to your will.

As thought is the most powerful agent in your life, provided you know how to develop and use it, never let the power of your thought be diluted by mixing with weak-minded or negative people—unless you are very strong-minded and can instead strengthen those persons. The weak should seek the company of those who are stronger. People who have no self-control should associate with those who are self-disciplined—the greedy man, for example, should eat with the man of self-control; with such an example before him, he will begin to reason, "I can also control my appetite."

Affirm Your True Nature

Just as by the power of thought you can change yourself to be whatever you want to be, so most importantly, you can change your consciousness from that of a mortal to a divine being. The mortal person is one who thinks, "This is the way I live and this is the way I will be until I die." But the divine person says, "I dreamt I was a mortal, but now I am awake and know that I am a child of God, made in the image of the Father." Though it takes time to realize this fully, it can be done.

If, when time comes for meditation at night, you yield to the thought, "It is too late now to meditate; let me sleep and I will meditate tomorrow," you will be sleeping on into the grave. When the world has surrendered to the drug of slumber, you be awake in God. And throughout the day's activities, think that it is God who is working through you. Give the responsibility to Him. He who thinks of God all the time, can he do wrong? Even if he happens to err, God knows it was his wish to do right. Give everything to God, and you will change because then the human ego can no longer dictate to you.

No matter what comes to you, just say, "God knows best. It is He who is giving me this suffering; it is He who is making me happy." With this attitude, all your nightmares of life will change into a beautiful dream of God.

Darkness is the absence of light. Delusion is darkness; Reality is light. Your eyes of wisdom are closed, so you see only the darkness; and you are suffering in that delusion. Change your consciousness, open your eyes and you will see in the stars the sparkle of that divine Light. In every atom of space you will see the twinkle of God's light of laughter. Behind every thought you shall feel the ocean of His wisdom.

The dance of life and death, and prosperity and failure, have no reality except as dreams of God. Realize this, and you shall see that it is materialized thoughts that are dancing around you, and that you are the ocean of thought. Nothing can stay nor hurt you.

Now I ask you to close your eyes and think of one bad habit you want to get rid of. If you concentrate with me as I say the words in Spirit, and you believe, you shall be free of that habit. Throw away the thought that you cannot give up whatever it is. I am sending a strong thought into your consciousness that right now you are rid of that habit. Affirm with me, "I am free of that habit now! I am free!" Hold on to that thought of freedom; forget the bad habit. Many of you will find that the habit you have willed away will never come back again.

Repeat after me, "I shall remold my consciousness. In this new year I am a new person. And I shall change my consciousness again and again until I have driven away all the darkness of ignorance, and manifested the shining light of Spirit in whose image I am made."

XII

Thoughts and Health

by Jayesh Nishar

A month ago, as a medical student in a hospital, I came across a most interesting case. One that I shall remember for a long time. Mr. Patel and Mr. Gupta were admitted within a few days of each other. Both suffered from a breathing disorder, asthma, but their outlooks on life were poles apart.

Mr. Patel took life in his stride. He was the sort of person who would always look at the brighter side of things. In fact, he once jokingly told me that his hospital stay was good in a way—at least he was getting a short vacation.

But Mr. Gupta was different. When he smelt flowers, he would look around for a coffin. He knew the price of everything and the value of nothing. He always grumbled about how bad the world was and how it was out to get him. He once remarked that the problem with the world was that there were very few people as broad-minded as he was. He could not sleep at night because he worried about everything and then he worried about the fact that he could not sleep.

After seven days, Mr. Patel was discharged hale and hearty while Mr. Gupta languished for two months. This somewhat exaggerated example focuses on a revolutionary concept in modern medicine. For long we have accepted the phrase, "A healthy mind in a healthy body," and that physical health is a prerequisite for peace of mind. But now there is compelling evidence to suggest that things may be the other way around. That it is our thoughts that exert a significant influence on health.

Our brain is a complex network of interacting chemicals called "neurotransmitters," the so-called messengers of the nervous system. A series of experiments have proven beyond doubt that the way we think changes the quality and quantity of these chemicals. These exert their actions on the organic systems of our body, the result being a change in our health.

The Fighting Spirit

One study on cancer patients has shown that those with a fighting spirit live as much as eight to ten years more than those without. Another study focuses on personality traits. It has been found that people who bottle up their anger are at a higher risk of suffering from peptic ulcers.

These are not isolated examples, but part of a whole new science called psycho-immunology, the relation between thoughts and the body's immune system. In fact, some psychiatrists emphatically stress that our thoughts are responsible for our health.

The message is clear. If we are aiming for a healthy body, the best of diets and exercise are not enough. We have to go deeper into the mysteries of the mind. We must discipline our mind to be happy. We know that happiness or sorrow are nothing but reactions of the mind to external stimuli. So if we can train our mind to react positively to any situation, then happiness will be ours. We do not have to hunt for happiness in the world outside, but rather, we must redirect our search to the world within. Once the mind is at peace, there is no doubt that it will exert a positive influence upon our health. For, as Edward Dyer says, "My mind to me is a kingdom with such pleasant joys therein I find that it excels all other bliss that earth affords or grows. Happy days are here again. Healthy days are here again."

XIII

A New Dimension of Being

by Vimala Thakar

If man only knew how to learn the greatest art of living! If he only knew how to live, to pass through various experiences without allowing any experience, pleasurable or painful, to leave a scratch on the consciousness! After all, every memory is a scratch on the consciousness. Consciousness gets mutilated. It is a bleeding and mutilated consciousness that we are carrying. There are scratches and scars of pleasurable and painful experiences, the memory of which we are carrying from one day to another. Through untold centuries, man has been carrying this burden. Now is the time to throw it off.

If we want real relationships as far as human beings are concerned, if man wants to learn the art of getting related to his fellows, he will have to leave the prison house that ego has created for him. He will have to step out of this vicious circle of responding through memory. That, for me, is the crux of the whole issue. That is the nature of the challenge. When we say that we have to find out if there is anything beyond the present consciousness, that we must step out of the psyche, it is nothing mysterious or mystical. There is nothing very difficult or extraordinary about it. A scientific approach to the human mind tells me very vividly that this is a mechanistic activity. So if anger, jealousy, envy, greed, or ambition come up, I do not identify myself with them and say "I am ambitious," or "I am angry, I am jealous." I do not act out of that identification, but I take distance from the reaction that is coming up, knowing that it is the product of collective humanity. We have to fight not only the outer symptoms of vested interests and structures; the real structure to be fought is inside.

It seems to me that one has to realize it as a fact of life that mental action is not going to help us in creating a new society. I wonder if you have noticed how people in the communist world tried to create a classless society, a society without exploitation. There was a noble dream of wiping out the state boundaries, and so on. And, very frankly, what does one find? One finds that the petty human mind is just the same there, as it is here. The relationship to money is the same. The ambition to acquire more and more money and store it is the same. Not for providing the basic needs—for providing the needs, money is necessary—but one earns much more, out of greed than for the need. Thus the relationship to money, property, the lust for ownership, the competition for power, fame, prestige, social emulation—everything is just the same as it is in other countries.

So altering the old structure cannot logically or naturally bring about a real change. One has to work on both fronts simultaneously. And in order to work simultaneously on both fronts, one has to begin with one's own psyche and try to explore a totally new dimension where the touch of the past will not pollute the living present. Each one must see this as the nature of the challenge, not seeing it while sitting in a quiet corner of the house, but seeing it while one is moving and working in the office, traveling in a bus, cooking a meal at home or talking to children in the school. One has to observe the movement of one's psyche in day-to-day life, see the mechanistic nature *there*, not treating the mechanistic nature as a new acquisition and storing it in the memory again—not that! One has to see it as a fact in daily relationships. That is the beauty of human relationships—they are the mirrors in which we can find out the quality of our inner life. We may indulge in wishful thinking and have very noble images of ourselves, but when we are exposed to a variety of temperamental idiosyncrasies, the vagaries of the human mind, we will see very clearly for ourselves how our actions are regulated, controlled, and directed by the impulses, the passions—you know, the whole momentum of the subconscious.

Meditation in Life

So meditation for such a revolutionary person is the most revolutionary action in life. It is the only total action. Everything else is fragmentary. Meditation is a way of life and not an act of the will. Not that one sits down and meditates in a corner! The revolutionary person will live the meditative way. He will watch and observe the movement of the psyche in him and try to find out how one can step out of it now and here. Not in isolation. There is no life in isolation. Life is in relationship. Relationships are inevitable for human beings. When the momentum comes up, one does not identify with it, but allows it to be exposed to the light of awareness. We have not done it. As soon as anger, or jealousy comes up, we either identify ourselves with it and act out of that identification, or we try to condemn it, suppress it, push it back, hide it or cover it up. These are the two ways we live. And then outwardly we try to be so-called courteous, polite with one another. Politeness becomes the mask—concealing the hypocrisy. Of course we do not like to call it hypocrisy; we are civilized people. We do not like to confess it even to ourselves. That is how it goes. Either people condemn it outright and try to suppress the mind and thereby become hypocrites; or we identify ourselves with it, and in the name of so-called spontaneity, act out of that.

To me, meditation is the third way out. The other two are only escapes from the fact. The meditative way is the way to understand the nature of mental action, that is, the movement of the ego, and not to identify oneself with it. You and I cannot do away with this psyche, the conscious, the subconscious, the unconscious—you know, the whole of it. We cannot destroy it; we cannot wish it away. We cannot fight it out. It is going to be there. If we allow it to be exposed to the light of awareness, that moment loses its grip on our consciousness, it loses its grip on us. It loses its hold because we see the objective and the subjective simultaneously, and in that perception of totality the consciousness has already taken off to a different plane altogether.

Effortless Transcendence

Thus we do not have to make an effort to transcend the content of the psyche. The very understanding, the very perception, results in an effortless transcendence. This has been witnessed in the lives of even ordinary human beings. This is not being advocated as a theory to you. It would be presumptuous on my part to waste your time in advocating or propagating theories. Transcendence of the psyche is a by-product of the understanding of the nature of the psyche. The understanding of its nature is the real action, if it is not theoretical. You know what academic knowledge does, don't you? When I was at the university, I must have read and studied books on so many subjects—philosophy, psychology, logic, ethics and metaphysics, and what not. But all my acquisition was related to the motive of passing the examination. And as soon as the examination was over I forgot everything. After a few weeks when I was asked a question about my studies, I said, "Oh, that is all over!" It just fell through the sieve of my memory because my acquisition of the knowledge was riding on the motive. The motive was providing the momentum to my acquisition. The motive was to pass an examination.

So, if we know, if we understand the mechanistic nature of brain and cerebral activity as a fact, then obviously there is no more identification with anything that mind brings up, except for the realm of engineering, science or technology, where you are dealing with certain static data. My information about a chair is valid today, it will be valid tomorrow, it will be valid after a year. But my knowledge about you or my experience with you may not be valid even after a week, because you may have changed in that week, you may have even changed in twenty-four hours. Human beings are extremely unpredictable. So if I try to store into memory my experience with you today and regard it valid for my relationship with you tomorrow, I have an unscientific, outmoded method of functioning in human relationships. Meditation is the way of getting free of memory in human relationships and having a consciousness which is ever innocent, ever fresh, that is, of living in a dimension of humility.

I know this is going to be very difficult, as then there will be no scope for the luxury of gossiping. There will be no indulgence in scandalizing. Human beings are ever-changing. And, yet, the time we waste in gossiping, in scandalizing, formulating opinions, and passing them on to others! Of course, newspapers will lose many of their sensational and thrilling items, because man will not pay attention to all that! If we see the implications of setting oneself free from this infatuation with the mind, getting beyond this phase of worshiping the mind, the implications are going to be very far-reaching. They are going to be far-reaching not only in space and time, but they will go deeper and deeper and percolate to the deepest layer of being. So transcendence of the psyche is not a result of human effort. It is a logical and natural consequence of understanding the truth.

After all, what is liberation? Understanding the nature of bondage results in liberation. If someone says that you have to understand what bondage is and then make an independent effort to get free, that person is talking in a rather light vein. He has not experimented. Spirituality is an experimental science. It is not a speculative game. If a person experiments and sees the movement, understands the nature of bondage as a fact, all the identification with it drops away gracefully, like an autumn leaf falling down from a tree without causing any injury or damage to the tree—just floating down, giving place to the new leaf to come up.

73

XIV

Sincerity and Total Involvement

by Swami Chinmayananda

The mind is the instrument through which we can make an effort to uncover the Truth. As long as the mind's attention is turned toward worldly objects, however, it will not be available for this higher pursuit. The mind, being extremely dynamic, functions constantly. All aesthetics, such as religious ceremonies, music, dance, expressive paintings, and the beauty of nature, are helpful in taking the mind away from the world. After having removed the mind from the outer world, we need to give it ample work to do in the inner world. It is for this reason that we keep the inward-turned mind occupied in *japa* (repetition of the Lord's name), chanting, meditation, and devotional singing (*kirtan*).

During *kirtan*, we must learn to sing with the whole mind. When the leader sings, sing mentally with him or her, and then repeat loudly. The effect of *kirtan* is not fully realized when we just sing mechanically. This is why some people become disenchanted with and then give up spiritual practices, as they have not felt their effectiveness. Singing *kirtan* is not an exercise for the throat, it is meant to discipline the mind.

It is said in the *Ramayana* that when Hanuman was lying unconscious, every hair on his body was heard whispering the name of Rama. This illustrates how Hanuman's mind was always totally absorbed in the singing of Rama's name. Anyone who chants with their entire mind enters a state of ecstasy, just like Chaitanya Mahaprabhu. Such a person has a profound influence on everyone.

When we sing, we produce vibrations in the atmosphere, and this can be considered as our contribution to benefit society and all living creatures. But what we sing with every cell in our body, and our entire mind, trains and benefits us. Modern psychiatry has proven that when the mind is disturbed, the body's chemistry is also disturbed. A mind absorbed in devotional chanting is a mind ready to come under our control. Then to transcend the mind is only another step. After withdrawing the mind from the world, we need to reflect inwardly and chant the mantra with our whole mind in an attitude of devotion. When we thus involve the mind, and surrender with deep devotion, the mind is brought back to us and reflection becomes easy. It is only when the mind is totally involved that one can realize the transcendental Truth. It is not merely an intellectual appreciation, nor sounds created by chanting.

Mental Images

The mind is thought-flow. Subjectively a thought is not possible without a mental image. If someone tries to convey a thought or an idea to us and an image does not arise, we ask several questions until an image appears in our mind. Thus, "thought" is a mental image, and a series of images arising and disappearing is called the mind. Mind is not a thing, power, or force, but only a function.

An appropriate word that could be created in context with the mind is "imagification." When we sit for meditation, we become especially aware of the images that our mind produces. We create these images ourselves and then we cry, "My mind is so agitated and I cannot transcend it." We limit ourselves by our own indiscriminate thoughts!

This is the reason our rishis have called all this a delusion.

We create a thought disturbance in ourselves, the Pure Consciousness, which is then called the individual mind or *jīva*. When we look through this disturbance, we see the world of plurality (*jagat*). Then we want to know who created the world, and presuppose a Creator (*Īśvara*). This individual-world-Lord (*Jīva-Jagat-Īśvara*) is all a creation of our own mind, which is in us, the Pure Consciousness.

For example, say a person begins to scratch his arm. When he continues to do so it becomes a wound. When he continues further, the wound starts to bleed and he cries out in pain, yet he continues to scratch. Who can save such a person? The only remedy is to stop scratching and allow the wound to heal. Then the bleeding and the wound will disappear. Similarly, one should stop "imagificating." Once "imagification" is halted, even for a moment, one comes to recognize the Truth. Thereafter such an individual can come back to play in the world. He may seem to "imagificate," but even when such a person continues to act in the world as before, he is constantly aware of and lives in the Truth. He is said to be in the world but not of the world. This is called freedom of the soul and such a person has experienced true wisdom (*jñāna*).

To say that such a person is working is absurd. Because of the limitations of language we have to use these words. When we use the sentence, "He is dead," it is a complete sentence. All sentences need a subject. In this sentence, the subject is "he." If "he" is dead, "he" is not there and yet we have to say "he" is dead. What we mean by the word "he" is that he who was previously alive, is now dead. Similarly, when a realized person works, he seemingly acts in this world, but it is only an illusion.

The following example will illustrate this point: Picture a huge ugly rock (the mind). After an earthquake, a spring suddenly rises out from behind, crosses over, and falls on the other side of the rock. After that, only the spring will be seen and it will hide the ugly rock within itself. Similarly, once the infinite divine flow of Consciousness floods out of oneself, it covers up the mind and body. The gross body may continue, but it will not be seen. It will be covered and only the Divine will flood out. It is just like when we wake up from a dream, there is nothing that has to be done to get rid of the dream, it just disappears. There is no magic involved and no one else can help us, not even our teacher. The secret is sincerity and total involvement. Develop sincerity from the core of your heart, and success will surely follow. All-blissful peace is the goal. Hurry Home!

PART FOUR

Reveling Within

*Go deep,
very deep down in the silence of your heart,
and you will find the Lord there
radiant and merciful.*

The Mother

Meditation means a finer province of thought. Thought can break through everything. The reason that thought does not reveal to us is because something is constantly cutting in on it. Only when our whole nature becomes silent, free from pretense, free from demand and discontent, can we have the steadiness of mind necessary for communion with the Ideal. We must express God-like qualities in our daily actions, if we would recognize His voice and perceive His presence.

Swami Paramananda
Daily Thoughts and Prayers

Thus we pass to the center of our silence. The will is at its highest activity. As an insect poised in the air, seemingly motionless, with wings in such rapid motion that they are invisible, is all the while sustained by its resistance to the air, so the will in this listening is not passive. It holds fast to its rest in God by sustained resistance to all that would drag it down or invade its silence. This is far from making the mind a blank. It is the filling of the mind with God to the exclusion of all else.

Quaker Practice of Silence

XV

The Path of Inquiry

by Ramana Maharshi

Q: What is the nature of the mind?

A: What is called the mind is a wondrous power residing in the Self. It causes all thought to arise. Apart from thought, there is no such thing as mind. Therefore, thought is the nature of mind. Apart from thoughts, there is no independent entity called the world. In the states of waking and dreaming, there are thoughts, as well as the world. Just as the spider emits the thread (of the web) out of itself and again withdraws it into itself, similarly, the mind projects the world out of itself and again resolves it into itself. When the mind comes out of the Self, the world appears. Therefore, when the world appears to be real, the Self does not appear; and when the Self appears (shines) the world does not appear. When one persistently inquires into the nature of the mind, the mind will end, leaving the Self as the residue. What is referred to as the Self is the *Ātman*. The mind always exists only in dependence on something gross; it cannot stay alone. It is the mind that is called the subtle body or the soul (*jīva*).

Q: What is the path of inquiry for understanding the nature of the mind?

A: That which rises as "I" in this body is the mind. If one inquires as to where in the body the thought "I" rises first, one would discover that it rises in the heart. That is the place of the mind's origin. Even if one thinks constantly "I," one will be led to that place. Of all the thoughts that arise in the mind, the "I" thought is the first. It is only after the rise of this that other thoughts arise. It is after the appearance of the first personal pronoun that the second and third personal pronoun appear; without the first personal pronoun there will not be the second and third.

Q: How will the mind become quiescent?

A: By the inquiry "Who am I?" This thought will destroy all other thoughts and like the stick used for stirring the burning pyre, it will itself, in the end, get destroyed. Then Self-realization will arise.

Persistent Inquiry

Q: What is the means for constantly holding on to the thought "Who am I?"

A: When other thoughts arise, one should not pursue them, but should inquire, "To whom did they arise?" It does not matter how many thoughts arise. As each thought arises, one should inquire with diligence, "To whom has this thought arisen?" The answer that would emerge would be, "To me." Then if one inquires "Who am I?" the mind will go back to its source, and the thought that arose will become quiescent. With repeated practice in this manner, the mind will develop the skill to stay in its source. When the mind that is subtle goes out through the brain and the sense organs, the gross names and forms appear. When it stays in the heart, the names and forms disappear.

Not letting the mind go out but retaining it in the Heart is what is called "inwardness." Letting the mind go out of the Heart is known as externalization. Thus, when the mind stays in the Heart, the "I" which is the source of all thoughts will go, and the Self that ever exists will shine. Whatever one does, one should do without the egoism of "I." If one acts in that way, all will appear as of the nature of Shiva (God).

Q: Are there no other means for making the mind quiescent?

A: Other than inquiry, there are no adequate means. If it is sought to control the mind through other means, the mind will appear to be controlled, but will again go forth. Through the control of breath also, the mind will become quiescent, but it will be quiescent only while the breath remains controlled. When the breath resumes, the mind also will again start moving and will wander as impelled by residual impressions.

The source is the same for both mind and breath. Thought, indeed, is the nature of the mind. The thought "I" is the first thought of the mind, and that is egoism. From this thought originates egoism and also the breath. Therefore, when the mind becomes quiescent, the breath is controlled; and when the breath is controlled, the mind becomes quiescent. But in deep sleep, although the mind becomes quiescent, the breath does not stop. This is because of the will of God, so that the body may be preserved and other people may not be under the impression that it is dead. In the state of waking and in *samādhi*, when the mind becomes quiescent, the breath is controlled. Breath is the gross form of mind. Till the time of death, the mind keeps breath in the body, and when the body dies, the mind takes the breath along with it. Therefore, the exercise of breath-control is only an aid for rendering the mind quiescent; it will not destroy the mind.

Like the practice of breath-control, meditation on the forms of God, repetition of mantras, restriction of food, and so on, are but aids for rendering the mind quiescent. Through meditation on the forms of God and through repetition of mantras, the mind becomes one-pointed. The mind will always be wandering. Just as when a chain is given to an elephant to hold in its trunk it will go along grasping the chain and nothing else. Similarly, when the mind is occupied with a name or form, it will grasp that alone. When the mind expands in the form of countless thoughts, each thought becomes weak; but as thoughts get resolved the mind becomes one-pointed and strong. Self-inquiry will become easy for such a mind. Of all the restrictive rules, that relating to the taking of *sattvic* food in moderate quantities is the best. By observing this rule, the *sattvic* quality of mind will increase, and that will be helpful to Self-inquiry.

Q: The residual impressions (thoughts) of objects appear unending like the waves of an ocean. When will all of them be removed?

A: As the meditation on the Self rises higher and higher the thoughts will get destroyed.

Q: Is it possible for the residual impressions of objects that come from beginningless time, as it were, to be resolved, and for one to remain as the pure Self?

A: Without yielding to the doubt, "Is it possible, or not?" one should persistently hold on to the meditation on the Self. Even if one is a great sinner, one should not worry and weep, "O I am a sinner, how can I be saved?" One should completely renounce the thought of, "I am a sinner" and concentrate keenly on meditation on the Self. Then one would surely succeed. There are not two minds; one good, and the other evil. The mind is only one. It is the residual impressions that are of two kinds—auspicious and inauspicious. When the mind is under the influence of auspicious impressions it is called good. And when it is under the influence of inauspicious impressions it is regarded as evil.

The mind should not be allowed to wander toward worldly objects and to the concerns of other people. However bad other people may appear to be, one should bear no hatred for them. Both desire and hatred should be eschewed. All that one gives to others one gives to oneself. If this truth is understood who will not give to others? When one's self arises, all arises; when one's self becomes quiescent all becomes quiescent. To the extent we behave with humility, to that extent the result will be good. If the mind is rendered quiescent, we may live anywhere.

The Truth of the Self

Q: How long should inquiry be practiced?

A: As long as there are impressions of objects in the mind, the inquiry of, "Who am I?" is required. As thoughts arise they should be destroyed right there in the very place of their origin, through inquiry. If one resorted to contemplation of the Self unintermittently, until the Self was gained, that alone would do. As long as there are enemies within the fortress, they will continue to come forth. If, on the other hand, they are destroyed as they emerge, the fortress will fall into our hands.

Q: What is the nature of the Self?

A: What exists in truth is the Self alone. The world, the individual soul, and God are appearances in it, like silver in mother-of-pearl; these three appear at the same time and disappear at the same time.

The Self is that where there is absolutely no "I" thought. That is called "Silence." The Self itself is the world; the Self itself is "I," the Self itself is God, all is Shiva, the Self.

Q: Is not everything the work of God?

A: Without desire, resolve, or effort, the sun rises. And in its mere presence, the sun-stone emits fire, the lotus blooms, water evaporates, and people perform their various functions and then rest. Just as in the presence of the magnet the needle moves, it is by virtue of the mere presence of God that the souls governed by the three (cosmic) functions or the fivefold divine activities perform their actions and then rest, in accordance with their respective karmas. God has no resolve; no karma attaches itself to Him. This is like worldly actions not affecting the sun, or like the merits and demerits of the other four elements not affecting the all-pervading ether.

Q: Of the devotees, who is the greatest?

A: He who gives himself up to the Self, that is God, is the most excellent devotee. Giving one's self up to God means remaining constantly in the Self without giving room for the rise of any thoughts other than the thought of the Self.

Whatever burdens are thrown on God, He bears them. Since the supreme power of God makes all things move, why should we, without submitting ourselves to it, constantly worry ourselves with thoughts about what should be done and how, and what should not be done and how not? We know that the train carries all loads, so after getting on it why should we carry our small luggage on our head to our discomfort, instead of putting it down in the train and feeling at ease?

Q: What is nonattachment?

A: As thoughts arise, destroying them utterly without any residue in the very place of their origin is nonattachment. Just as the pearl-diver ties a stone to his waist, sinks to the bottom of the sea and there takes the pearls, so each of us should be endowed with nonattachment, dive within oneself, and obtain the Self-Pearl.

Q: Is it not possible for God and the Guru to affect the release of a soul?

A: God and the Guru will only show the way to release; they will not by themselves take the soul to the state of release.

In truth, God and the Guru are not different. Just as the prey that has fallen into the jaws of the tiger has no escape, so those who have come within the ambit of the Guru's gracious look will be saved by the Guru and will not get lost. Yet, each should by his own effort pursue the path shown by God or Guru and gain release. One can know oneself only with one's eye of knowledge, and not with somebody else's. Does he who is Rama require the help of a mirror to know that he is Rama?

Q: Is it necessary for one who longs for release to inquire into the nature of the categories (*tattvas*)?

A: Just as one who wants to throw away garbage has no need to analyze it and see what it is, similarly one who wants to know the Self has no need to count the number of categories or to inquire into their characteristics. What he has to do is to reject altogether the categories that hide the Self, and the world should be considered like a dream.

Q: Is there any difference between waking and dreaming?

A: Waking is long, and a dream is short; other than this there is no difference. Just as waking happenings seem real while awake, so do those in a dream while dreaming. In the dream the mind takes on another body. In both waking and dream states, thoughts, names, and forms occur simultaneously.

Q: Is it any use reading books for those who long for release?

A: All the texts say that to gain release one should render the mind quiescent; therefore their conclusive teachings are that the mind should be rendered quiescent; once this has been understood there is no need for endless reading. In order to quieten the mind one has only to inquire within oneself what one's Self is; how could this search be done in books? One should know one's Self with one's own eye of wisdom. The Self is within the five sheaths; but books are outside them. Since the Self has to be inquired into by discarding the five sheaths, it is futile to search for it in books. There will come a time when one will have to forget all that one has learned.

The Source of Happiness

Q: What is happiness?

A: Happiness is the very nature of the Self; happiness and the Self are not different. There is no happiness in any object of the world. We imagine, through our ignorance, that we derive happiness from objects. When the mind goes out, it experiences misery. In truth, when its desires are fulfilled, it returns to its own place and enjoys the happiness that is the Self.

Similarly, in the states of sleep, *samādhi*, and fainting, and when the desired object is obtained or the disliked object is removed, the mind becomes inward-turned, and enjoys pure Self-happiness. Thus the mind moves without rest, alternately going out of the Self and returning to it. Under the tree, the shade is pleasant; out in the open the heat is scorching. A person who has been going out in the sun feels cool when he reaches the shade. Someone who keeps on going from the shade into the sun and then back into the shade is a fool. A wise man stays permanently in the shade.

In the same way, the mind of the one who knows the truth does not leave *Brahman*. The mind of the ignorant, on the contrary, revolves in the world, feeling miserable, and for some time returns to *Brahman* to experience happiness. In fact, what is called the world is only thought. When the world disappears, that is, when there is no thought, the mind experiences happiness, and when the world appears it goes through misery.

Q: What is wisdom insight (*jñāna-dṛṣṭi*)?

A: Remaining quiet is what is called wisdom-insight. To remain quiet is to resolve the mind in the Self. Telepathy, knowing the past, present, and future happenings and clairvoyance do not constitute wisdom-insight.

Q: What is the relation between desirelessness and wisdom?

A: Desirelessness is wisdom. The two are not different; they are the same. Desirelessness is refraining from driving the mind toward any object. Wisdom means the appearance of no object. In other words, not seeking what is other than the Self is detachment or desirelessness; not leaving the Self is wisdom.

Q: What is the difference between inquiry and meditation?

A: Inquiry consists in retaining the mind in the Self. Meditation consists in thinking that one's Self is *Brahman,* Existence-Consciousness-Bliss.

Q: What is release?

A: Inquiring into the nature of one's Self that is in bondage, and realizing one's true nature is release.

XVI

The Highest Truth

by Swami Chinmayananda

Poets in their poetic moods, scientists in their laboratory, artists at their work—all of them discover a joy that is not typical of what we usually experience in the mind. This joy arises subjectively from the steadiness of the mind. Despite this steadiness and no matter how noble the thoughts, the mind continues to exist. And as long as the mind survives, thought-agitations veil the Self under a mist of mind-created confusions. This mind is the cause for nonapprehension of the real Essence in us. Therefore, the mind is to be completely sublimated.

That which is called as *Brahman*, tmaṇSelf, the Reality, is nothing other than mindlessness. As long as there is a mind, *Brahman* or Reality cannot be experienced. Where the mind has ended, that itself is *Brahman*.

Veils of the Mind

When we look at an object through our mind, we never see the object as it is. We always see it colored through our mind. One who does not have right knowledge can look, but does not see. He sees only his own projection.

Look at a flower and write down the thoughts that come into your mind. "It is a beautiful flower. It is yellow in color. Its name is such and such." If you know botany, you know to which family it belongs. "I have seen such a flower at my friend's place.

It was in that city, in his house." And so it continues. What are you thinking? You are now thinking about your friend. Though you are looking at a flower, you do not see the flower. It is only a springboard for the mind to wander.

If you can see the flower as it is, you see only *Brahman.* Remove quality, activity, adjectives, and relationship and then look at the flower; what you see is nothing but *Brahman.* Mind is only because of these four things. These four are interpretations of the mind, and wherever the mind functions, it functions in these four spheres only. Mind sees the quality, or it starts thinking in terms of its activity, name, or relationship, and therefore you do not see the flower.

Try to see a flower or a blade of grass as it is. Do not name it. Remove the four thought-modifications, and look at them. Look at any object, whether it is a person or the whole universe. If these four thought-modifications are not there, the mind has ended. All these four are nothing but interpretations—prattlings of the mind. Remove them and look, there is nothing but alertness or consciousness.

Mind at this alertness is the mind at meditation. Mind at meditation is no longer a mind. As long as we are identified with the mind, we are far, far away from the Reality. The moment you forget that mind, you are That. *Tat Tvam Asi.* This is maximum evolution.

The Challenge

To transcend the mind is the challenge that is to be faced. One has to grow to become a God-man. In order to achieve this we have to stop the play of the mind. A fraction of a second is enough; you do not have to stay there for long. After thus knowing the real and wider capability of your true nature, play with the mind. There will be a new sense of freedom in all your activities because you will know that you are not these limitations. You do not belong to them and they do not belong to you. We are only sojourners here. We are natives of a completely different realm. In that way if we look at any fleecy cloud, any twinkling star, any winged butterfly, any nodding leaf, each object is but a springboard for us to rocket ourselves into that ecstatic experience of the Highest.

Any method by which the range of the mind's activities can be reduced is called *sādhana*. Activities such as reading scriptures, Gita chanting, serving the poor, political involvement, or looking after our family all can be considered good, as they help prevent the mind from getting dissipated in various other fields. The process by which the mind can be annihilated at the body level is *karma* yoga (the path of selfless action). The process by which the mind can be transcended at the mental level is called *bhakti* yoga (the path of devotion), and at the intellectual level it is *jñāna* yoga (the path of knowledge). All of these yogas are processes by which the mind can be transcended.

To rediscover our own Self is the culmination of evolution. It brings total contentment—a complete sense of fulfillment. To experience this is the goal. Listen, reflect, meditate, and come to apprehend that "I am Shiva," that spiritual Essence alone. Only when we come to experience it will we understand.

The no-mind state is the experience of pure Awareness, with no distracting thoughts, only the infinite changeless Self. This is the goal to be reached, the Truth to be realized, the experience divine to be lived as the meditator's own essential Self. It is not a thing to be objectively recognized or even intellectually comprehended. This state is to be spiritually apprehended, as an immediate, personal, inner experience. In this state meditation gets fulfilled, and the meditator becomes the one Self, where the triple factors, meditator-meditated-meditation, coalesce to become one vital experience of total transcendental awakening, or Self-realization.

XVII

Bringing the Mind Home

by Sogyal Rinpoche

In meditation, as in all arts, there has to be a delicate balance between relaxation and alertness. Once a monk called Shrona was studying meditation with one of the Buddha's closest disciples. He had difficulty finding the right frame of mind. He tried very hard to concentrate, and gave himself a headache. Then he relaxed his mind, but so much that he fell asleep. Finally he appealed to Buddha for help. Knowing that Shrona had been a famous musician before he became a monk, Buddha asked him: "Weren't you a *vina* player when you were a layperson?"

Shrona nodded.

"How did you get the best sound out of your vina? Was it when the strings were very tight or when they were very loose?"

"Neither. When they had just the right tension, neither too taut nor too slack."

"Well, it is exactly the same with your mind."

One of the greatest of Tibet's many woman masters, Ma Chik Lap Drön, said: "Alert, alert; yet relax, relax. This is a crucial point for the View in meditation." Alert your alertness, but at the same time be relaxed, so relaxed in fact that you don't even hold onto an idea of relaxation.

When people begin to meditate, they often say that their

thoughts are running riot, and have become wilder than ever before. But I reassure them and say that this is a good sign. Far from meaning that your thoughts have become wilder, it shows that *you* have become quieter, and you are finally aware of just how noisy your thoughts have always been. Don't be disheartened or give up. Whatever arises, just keep being present, keep returning to the breath, even in the midst of all the confusion.

In the ancient meditation instructions, it is said that at the beginning thoughts will arrive one on top of another uninterrupted, like a steep mountain waterfall. Gradually, as you perfect meditation, thoughts become like the water in a deep, narrow gorge, then a great river slowly winding its way down to the sea, and finally the mind becomes like a still and placid ocean, ruffled by only the occasional ripple or wave.

Sometimes people think that when they meditate there should be no thoughts and emotions at all; and when thoughts and emotions do arise, they become annoyed and exasperated with themselves and think they have failed. Nothing could be further from the truth. There is a Tibetan saying: "It is a tall order to ask for meat without bones, and tea without leaves." So long as you have a mind, there will be thoughts and emotions.

Just as the ocean has waves, or the sun has rays, so the mind's own radiance is its thoughts and emotions. The ocean has waves, yet the ocean is not particularly disturbed by them. The waves are the *very nature* of the ocean. Waves will rise, but *where* do they go? Back into the ocean. And where do the waves come from? The ocean. In the same manner, thoughts and emotions are the radiance and expression of the *very nature* of the mind. They rise from the mind, but where do they dissolve? Back into the mind. Whatever rises, do not see it as a particular problem. If you do not impulsively react, if you are only patient, it will once again settle into its essential nature.

When you have this understanding, then rising thoughts only enhance your practice. But when you do not understand what they intrinsically are—the radiance of the nature of your mind—then your thoughts become the seed of confusion. So have a spacious, open, and compassionate attitude toward your thoughts and emotions, because in fact your thoughts are your family, the family of your mind. Before them, as Dudjom Rinpoche used to say: "Be like an old wise man, watching a child play."

The Spaciousness of Meditation

We often wonder what to do about negativity or certain troubling emotions. In the spaciousness of meditation, you can view your thoughts and emotions with a totally unbiased attitude. When your attitude changes, then the whole atmosphere of your mind changes, even the very nature of your thoughts and emotions. When *you* become more agreeable, then *they* do; if you have no difficulty with them, they will have no difficulty with you either.

So whatever thoughts and emotions arise, allow them to rise and settle, like the waves in the ocean. Whatever you find yourself thinking, let that thought rise and settle, without any constraint. Don't grasp at it, feed it, or indulge it; don't cling to it and don't try to solidify it. Neither follow thoughts nor invite them; be like the ocean looking at its own waves, or the sky gazing down on the clouds that pass through it.

You will soon find that thoughts are like the wind; they come and go. The secret is not to "think" about thoughts, but to allow them to flow through the mind, while keeping your mind free of afterthoughts.

In the ordinary mind, we perceive the stream of thoughts as continuous; but in reality this is not the case. You will discover for yourself that there is a gap between each thought. When the past thought is past, and the future thought has not yet arisen, you will always find a gap in which the Rigpa, the nature of mind, is revealed. So the work of meditation is to allow thoughts to slow down, to make that gap become more and more apparent.

My master had a student called Apa Pant, a distinguished Indian diplomat and author, who served as Indian ambassador in a number of capital cities around the world. He had even been the representative of the Government of India in Tibet in Lhasa, and for a time he was their representative in Sikkim. He was also a practitioner of meditation and yoga, and each time he saw my master, he would always ask him "how to meditate." He was following an Eastern tradition, where the student keeps asking the master one simple, basic question, over and over again.

Apa Pant told me this story. One day our master Jamyang Khyentse was watching a "Lama Dance" in front of the Palace Temple in Gangtok, the capital of Sikkim, and he was chuckling at the antics of the *atsara*, the clown who provides light relief between dances. Apa Pant kept pestering him, asking him again and again how to meditate, so this time when my master replied, it was in such a way as to let him know that he was telling him once and for all: "Look, it's like this: When the past thought has ceased, and the future thought has not yet risen, isn't there a gap?"

"Yes," said Apa Pant.

"Well, prolong it: *That* is meditation."

Various Pitfalls

As you continue to practice, you may have all kinds of experiences, both good and bad. Just as a room with many doors and windows allows the air to enter from many directions, in the same way, when your mind becomes open, it is natural that all kinds of experiences can come into it. You might experience states of bliss, clarity, or absence of thoughts. In one way these are very good experiences, and signs of progress in meditation. For when you experience bliss, it is a sign that desire has temporarily dissolved. When you experience real clarity, it's a sign that aggression has temporarily ceased. When you experience a state of absence of thought, it's a sign that your ignorance has temporarily died. By themselves they are good experiences, but if you get attached to them they become obstacles. Experiences are not realization in themselves, but if we remain free of attachment to them, they become what they really are, that is, materials for realization.

Negative experiences are often the most misleading because we usually take them as a bad sign. But in fact the negative experiences in our practice are blessings in disguise. Try not to react to them with aversion as you might normally do, but recognize them instead for what they truly are, merely experiences, illusory and dream-like. The realization of the true nature of the experience liberates you from the harm or danger of the experience itself, and as a result even a negative experience can become a source of great blessing and accomplishment. There are innumerable stories of how masters worked like this with negative experiences and transformed them into catalysts for realization.

Traditionally it's said that for a real practitioner, it's not the negative experiences but the good ones that bring obstacles. When things are going well, you have got to be especially careful and mindful so that you don't become complacent or overconfident. Remember what Dudjom Rinpoche said to me when I was in the middle of a very powerful experience: "Don't get too excited. In the end, it's neither good nor bad." He knew I was becoming attached to the experience: *that* attachment, like any other, has to be cut through. What we have to learn, in both meditation and in life, is to be free of attachment to the good experiences, and free of aversion to the negative ones.

Dudjom Rinpoche warns us of another pitfall: "On the other hand, in meditation practice, you might experience a muddy, semiconscious, drifting state, like having a hood over your head: a dreamy dullness. This is really nothing more than a kind of blurred and mindless stagnation. How do you get out of this state? Alert yourself, straighten your back, breathe the stale air out of your lungs, and direct your awareness into clear space to freshen your mind. If you remain in this stagnant state, you will not evolve; so whenever this setback arises, clear it again and again. It is important to be as watchful as possible, and to stay as vigilant as you can."

Whatever method you use, drop it, or simply let it dissolve on its own, when you find you have arrived naturally at a state of alert, expansive, and vibrant peace. Then continue to remain there quietly, undistracted, without necessarily using any particular method. The method has already achieved its purpose. However, if you do stray or become distracted, then return to whatever technique is most appropriate to call you back.

The real glory of meditation lies not in any method but in its continual living experience of presence, in its bliss, clarity, peace, and most important of all, complete absence of grasping. The diminishing of grasping in yourself is a sign that you are becoming freer of yourself. And the more you experience this freedom, the clearer the sign that the ego and the hopes and fears that keep it alive are dissolving, and the closer you will come to the infinitely generous "wisdom of egolessness." When you live in that wisdom home, you'll no longer find a barrier between "I" and "you," "this" and "that," "inside" and "outside," you'll have come, finally, to your true home, the state of non-duality.

XVIII

The Art of Meditation

by Swami Chinmayananda

Meditation is an effortless state where all actions cease. To reach this state, however, various spiritual practices are necessary to help control, regulate, and redirect the thought-processes. Mind is thought-flow; from these thoughts our entire world is projected; and this flow has to be dried up. A complete drying-up is not possible right away, but the direction of the flow can be changed. At this moment, our mind is oriented toward the external world of sense objects. To turn it toward the spring of Consciousness in ourselves is the aim of meditation.

Processes to meditation are not meditation. Truly speaking, meditation can never be a verb. It is always a noun. As long as it is a verb, that is, as long as we are trying to meditate, it is only a *sādhana* (spiritual practice). When we reach the *sādhya* (the end or goal) it becomes a noun.

The masters of meditation, the great rishis, have given us elaborate instructions on how we can slowly train the mind. They gave us various techniques by which our thoughts can be brought into complete harmony until ultimately all thoughts cease. We then come to recognize the very Source from which all thoughts arise. To cease the process of thinking is to end the mind. When the mind has collapsed the individuality ceases. "I," the individual, wakes up at that moment to a new dimension of the Infinite. It is a state that cannot be explained; it has to be experienced.

The scriptures that indicate this pure state of Being are the Upanishads. When reading the Upanishads some of us come to the erroneous conclusion that since we already are That, we only need to read the scriptures, but this is not sufficient. It has to be brought into our direct experience. To make it our experience we have to train the mind, and persuade it in a number of ways to become quiet. These efforts constitute *jñāna sādhana*, which is loosely translated as meditation. Since we have to transcend that very same mind that constantly functions through the body, the mind has to be reigned in away from the body. This involves much effort, for it is the nature of the mind to experience the world through the sense organs. If these experiences are joyous, we will seek to repeat them. Thus the identification of the mind with the body has become very strong and to stop identifying with the body is not easy; the mind will offer great resistance.

In deep sleep the mind dissociates from the physical body and is completely relaxed. There is no awareness of the body. That is why as a preliminary step, the meditator is advised to learn the technique of sitting motionless and quiet. The longer one sits without any motion, the more the body disappears from our awareness. As the body disappears from our consciousness we feel great peace and bliss. But even though peace and joy may be experienced, it is a kind of dull quietude, not elevating or enriching. There is a quietness, no doubt, but a dry quietude of the scalding desert, not the magnificent quietude that one experiences in the grandeur of a forest. The mind can develop enormous mental vitality, and because of its high degree of concentration can even develop mystical powers. With this quiet, concentrated mind one can gain much material success. But it does not have the divine potential to transmute our very existence and character. This can happen only when we enter the inner kingdom of Self-discovery. To convert the dry silence into something noble becomes the spiritual path. To learn the art of meditation, experienced masters advise a number of physical and mental adjustments.

Helpful Hints

First, learn to sit quietly, and not with a full stomach. A yogi only fills half of his stomach with food. One quarter is filled with water and one quarter remains empty. The sitting must not be done soon after a heavy meal. Meditation is always better when digestion and assimilation have been completed. The accomplished meditator eats only once a day, or else eats very small quantities two or three times a day so that the body is fed, but there is no load on it, and it is always available for higher purposes. One should recognize that the purpose of eating is solely to maintain fitness and good health.

The meditator is then advised to relax the body. Sitting in a comfortable seat, fingers interlocked, hands resting in the lap, see that the body is very still and erect. In this position of relaxation, you hang the physical body, as it were, upon a cross represented by the erect vertebral column and the collarbones. Just as one hangs one's coat on a coat-hanger. The gross weight and tensions of the body no longer pull your attention to the physical plane. You have entered the meditation seat, with all the preliminaries of body adjustment completed.

Fill the mind with joy. Smile from the mind and the heart, not from the lips only. See that the mind is surcharged with joy. It is not that we have no worries, we just do not carry these worries to the meditation seat. The worries are kept, along with the shoes, outside the meditation room. We are here to relax. We fill our minds with the joy of meeting our Beloved. Worries will be there for everyone. Refuse to recognize them, just as we reject them before sleeping. In this joyous attitude the mind is pliable. We can change its shape and contours. Even when we try to persuade other individuals to do something, we first try to make them happy before we put forth our request. With this quiet, cheerful mind, mentally prostrate to the teacher or Lord, surrendering the ego at His feet. "O Lord, lead me, guide me! I do not know where to go, all that I know is that this is not the way I want to continue to live." This process helps to eliminate the ego for a moment. Relax. Let go.

With this quiet mind, chant your favorite mantra continuously; and remain conscious of the mind chanting the mantra. An inspiring word, a divine verse, or a statement from the scripture becomes a mantra when it is repeated in the mind and we feel uplifted by it.

Out of the many chants and hymns available, select a favorite and let the mind become absorbed with its essential meaning. After that, hum the tune and chant it. As the mantra is being chanted in the mind, we become aware of the atmosphere of devotion that is created in ourselves. At the peak of this repetition, when we are extremely conscious of the chanting, the chanting is eventually brought down to a mental whisper. Ultimately, remove the mantra from the mind, and learn to be conscious of the remaining silence. When we are conscious of that silence, it is the highest point of mental tuning. Repeated practice can deepen this silence, and bring the mind into more and more quietude.

Maintaining a Devotional Attitude

Having brought the mind into this attitude of adoration for the Self, do not initiate any new thoughts. Come down from this state in steady, slow stages. To remain in that atmosphere of peace and devotion, every religion prescribes prayers, hymns, chants, and invocations that contain the qualities of the Lord and the glory of that state. Maintain the mind in that attitude as long as possible without hastening into the fields of action or work. Even after rising from the seat, move about in the house softly, and slowly continue with obligatory duties and responsibilities.

These attempts to quiet the mind are called meditation, but, in fact, they all are preparations for meditation. By themselves they do not constitute true meditation. In this quiet mind, emotionally charged with devotion for the Lord and completely surrendered, the ego is liquidated for the time being and the external world does not disturb us. We have now created the conducive quietude in the mind for the intellect to begin its inquiry into the various exercises in contemplation advised in the Upanishads and the *Bhagavad Gītā*.

As a result of these contemplations, a deeper and more dynamic silence is reached; a positive state of the Experience Divine, which accelerates in its momentum and dimension as the mind slows down. This cannot be achieved overnight. Initially it may seem difficult, but as time passes, we gain admission into these depths and become welcome guests.

When we first sit for meditation and start our *japa* (repetition of the Lord's name), there will be a tremendous rush of irrelevant thoughts. Many of us become disappointed at this stage. While preparing to enter the seat of meditation the mind was relatively peaceful. But the moment we sit, an inordinate number of thoughts arise in the mind. This is due to the subconscious mind throwing up its suppressions and repressions whenever the conscious mind becomes quiet. There are many varieties of thoughts gathered in our day-to-day contact with the world. They become lodged in the subconscious mind because they have not been dealt with, or completely digested. They cannot escape because of the conscious mind's constant engagement in gathering new experiences. As the conscious mind becomes quiet, the subconscious mind gets a chance to empty itself. At such moments we should not curse ourselves, but rather congratulate the mind for flushing itself out.

When these thoughts arise, sit and watch this parade of thoughts peacefully with serene composure. Do not identify with them. Do not become involved with them. It is the dirt that is being thrown out, it is the mind's vomit. Stand aside and just be an observer. Be aware of the thoughts, but do not try to classify or label them as good or bad. Let them be flushed out by themselves. When we thus stand as a witness, not involved in the quality or theme of those thoughts, the flood exhausts itself. Ignore them and repeat the Lord's name. The Lord's name is repeated so that we remain within ourselves. Let the thoughts come and go. They will.

When this flood finally ceases, we shall experience a great influx of peace and quietude in the mind. In that quiet, cheerful mind, invoke the Lord or the Teacher, prostrate to Him mentally, seeking His guidance and grace. In this peaceful mind, with as much devotion as you can muster, let your emotional nature become involved with all love and devotion in chanting the mantra, being aware only of each mantra rising and slowly disappearing into the mind. It is with this quiet mind that contemplation starts. Exercises in contemplation are described in all scriptures. By repeatedly thinking of these exercises, *saṁskāras* (impressions) are created in us. A mind rich in pure *saṁskāras* is of the nature of the Self, which is called Knowledge. That mind, when it is released from all other disturbances, is the one that has the sensitivity to experience the Self. The rishis recommended that exercises in contemplation be pursued with this quiet mind.

Entering Contemplation

The following contemplative lines can be used: "The sun illuminates the waves of the ocean, the waves of the ocean by themselves have no light. It is in the light of the sun that they are perceivable. Similarly, thoughts arise in the mind. By themselves they are matter, and therefore, not sentient. It is in the light of Consciousness that they are shining."

"The waves are only in the ocean, they cannot touch the sun. The sun illumines them. Likewise, agitations are only in the mind. They cannot touch Me. I am that pure Consciousness. *Śivoham, Śivoham*. I am blissful Consciousness, the most auspicious. Shiva am I."

If sleep overcomes you while trying to enter contemplation, try breathing out. Slowly breathe out the last bit of air in the lungs, and just keep it out. Tell the mind that it is welcome to sleep. Within half a minute, why, even ten seconds, the mind surrenders, and along with all the cells of the body requests your kind permission to continue breathing! Slowly start breathing in and fill the lungs again. Biologically, this hastens a little of the blood circulation; the pulse rate goes up, and with that, the gathering momentum of sleep slows down and evaporates. The mind is lifted. These are the sacred methods of the meditator to fight the inner battle. They will only have to be used in the early stages. Once we start to enjoy meditation and discover in ourselves an unearthly amount of peace and bliss, persuasion is no longer necessary as the mind runs toward it by itself.

When sitting quietly for meditation, thoughts will flow out due to the old *samskāras*. It is when the thoughts are rising repeatedly that we use our contemplative exercises to bring the mind back. Think along the following lines: "These thoughts are rising in infinite Consciousness. Whatever be the quality and theme of these thoughts, they cannot affect Me because I am the Consciousness that alone is. The Illuminator, the Subject, is different from the illuminated, the object." Thus, we go back into the state of pure Awareness. But if, instead, we protest against the rising thoughts, worry about their quality or become enchanted by their theme, we are identifying with the not-Self. At such moments, hold on to the pure Self. All the various explanations of the Self are exercises.

"The Knower am I. Everything else is known. I am the one Knower in all bodies. In Me, the Knower, there are no bodies. Since there are no bodies, I am within and without, everywhere, at all places. That infinite essence is the Lord, the absolute Reality. That is Me."

New students should not try to stay at this peak for too long, as this will create much suppression. A quick thrust, and an immediate retreat should be the attempt until we become drawn into it effortlessly. Meditation is a state where efforts must cease. If we try to remain there with effort, it is exhausting and will create suppression.

Remain Centered

Consciousness that illuminates the silence is the Self, the "I." This is Me. But unfortunately, as soon as a sound is heard, our mind evaluates it, labels it, and starts playing upon its significance due to past habits. The sound itself does not disturb us. Our mind running after the sound and starting a new procession of thoughts makes the mind roam about. The Consciousness, Me, riding on the mind, appears to be going away from the center. It is the perceiver-feeler-thinker that is disturbed when the mind is disturbed. Thus, step into the center and stay in the Self, watching and recognizing the intellectual, emotional, and physical equipments and their worlds.

"In all these movements I am the motionless center. I envelop them all with My Consciousness. By My grace they have the ability to move. These movements are only for My entertainment. I need not become involved with them. They change: I cannot change, the changeless light of Consciousness am I."

To make this contemplation effective, the inner personality is to be prepared. These preparations are called *bāhya sādhana*. When working and functioning in the world, the constant remembrance of the goal should be maintained in the mind. Instead of allowing an arrogant ego to override us, we should perform all duties in a spirit of surrender unto Him, ever acting as His instrument. Thus, the pure mind is identified with, and the agitations are exhausting themselves. For such a karma yogi it becomes easier to come to the seat of meditation with the right mental mood. Be firmly convinced that we are not trying to see something, to experience something, or to become something. We are trying to lift ourselves into a new dimension of existence where we are going to be what we are, not what we consider ourselves to be today—the wrappings of matter.

Developing attitudes of love, forgiveness, humility, surrender in our relationships with others, performing rituals, and practicing moral and ethical values—all these practices contribute to success in the seat of meditation. Once the mind is thus prepared, it is then applied in contemplation. We must reorient our entire attitude to life. It is not a state of dull stupor, but it is a ripened, positive state of Being, by whose grace the mind and intellect's expressions are possible.

The contemplative path is the product of a normal, healthy, dynamic life, not a sluggish, idle, and unproductive existence. Plenty of love, a quantum of work—almost to a suicidal degree—should be undertaken with the right attitude of pure love and devotion to the Self. Through intelligent study, regular practice, reflection, and discussing these matters with similar hearts, we train the mind. Try to fulfill duties as best as you know how, and learn to let go of what you cannot. Underneath the sorrows and tensions of existence, *vāsanās* (inherent tendencies) are functioning in their field. But keep in mind, "I am the Consciousness illumining them all." With this attitude, let them pass, never take them too seriously. When our life is thus focused toward the Higher, in a very short time, experiences of the Higher flood the soul.

Once we receive even a distant waft of this fragrance, the mind will refuse to enter into the outer world. Today, when we sit for meditation, the mind runs into the sense-world because in the past it discovered moments of joy there, however imperfect they may have been. But once the mind gets the flavor of the complete bliss of the Self, it will need much persuasion to make it come back into living a routine life.

Study of the scriptures is very important for meditation. When the mind is full of devotion and understanding, it discovers in itself the courage to leave the not-Self, and then the movement toward the Self is effortless. When we cannot sleep, it is because of our anxieties. Some people need to read in order to coach the mind to sleep, and others require music. But there are people who go to bed, lie down and immediately go to sleep. Analyze the state of sleep and you understand exactly what meditation is.

The cumulative effect of all *sādhana* is a good and honest life, so that when we sit for meditation the mind no longer wanders. Therefore, a chaste and honest life is a prerequisite. If we have compromised our ideals, the mind will be disturbed and becomes an obstacle in itself. This is the universal law.

Expect progressive development, not immediate rewards. At this moment our idea of progress is quite imaginary, as we do not really know what the goal is. Since we do not know the goal, we cannot judge our progress. One who says that he has been meditating but is not progressing, feels so only because he was not really meditating. Our progress is hindered when the mind is constantly calculating and evaluating. Meditate regularly and you will progress. Leave the results to Him. Remember Him, and strive on. Even a little meditation protects us from infinite fears. Slowly fold up the mind and unfold the Self. Always remember that we are performing a very delicate operation. The mind is very sensitive, more sensitive and softer than a flower. Do not exert any force upon it. Persuasion and knowledge are the safest methods. Lovingly lead the mind to the Sanctum Sanctorum.

XIX

The Loving Heart

by Swami Ranganathananda

I shall give you five verses from one of the greatest spiritual books of India, namely, the *Śrīmad Bhagavatam*, in which there is a passage expounding a calculus of man's spiritual growth and development (1:2:17-21). It begins with a reference to a spiritual practice common to many higher religions—Jewish, Hindu, Christian, Buddhist, Islamic—namely, repeating the name of God. What happens when we repeat the name of God with devotion in our hearts? That is described stage by stage in these verses:

> When the blessed divine Krishna, who lives in the hearts of all, hears the recitation of His name by the devotee, He gently wipes away all that is evil in the heart of the devotee, for He is the friend of all good people.

As the Hindus recite various names of God like Krishna, Shiva, Hari, and so on, in the Catholic church, there are mantras like Ave Maria, and other divine names in other religions. The verse says, God is the friend of the devotee, helping in his or her spiritual progress. The next verse says:

> When most of the impurities of the heart have been removed by the practice of constant devotion to God, man's *bhakti*, or devotion to God, the most excellent and Holy One, becomes steady (while it was unsteady before).

Mind is devoted to God at some time; it loses all interest in spiritual life at another time. This is the condition when one begins the spiritual life. But, at this stage, the devotion becomes steady, like the compass needle constantly pointing to the north. This is called *naiṣṭhikī-bhakti*, steady devotion. Sorrows and failures cannot affect that devotion to God. In many Christian saints also, we can study this kind of progress and development of steady devotion. That steadiness is the product of the purity of mind. What happens then? The next verse explains it in a wonderful way:

In that state (of steady devotion) the mind (of the devotee) becomes freed from the pressures of *rajas* (passion), and *tamas* (inertia) (forces of nature), and unsmitten by (their bitter fruits of) lust and greed and other passions, it becomes steady in the peace of *sattva* (purity and calmness).

Impelled by the forces of *rajas* and *tamas*, the mind becomes inclined to evil, to come under the influence of, what Vedanta calls, the six enemies of man: lust, anger, greed, delusion, arrogance, and violence. Free from these forces, the mind shines pure in *sattva*; it is the mind which is pure that can realize spirituality. Blessed are the pure in heart, for they shall see God, says Jesus. And so, the next verse says:

When the mind thus becomes tranquil (in *sattva*) through the practice of devotion to God, the devotee, who is now free from all sensory attachments experiences the truth of God.

The Consummation of Spiritual Life

And finally, what happens to the seeker through such realization? The last verse answers:

When the divine Lord is realized within oneself, all the knots of the heart are broken, all doubts get destroyed, and all ego-centered actions and their *saṁskāras* become eliminated.

These knots of the heart, what modern psychology calls complexes, become broken; too many complexes distort the human psyche, and complexes are formed when we do not have the spiritual strength to digest all experiences. When experiences digest man instead of man digesting his experiences; and that digestion is a function of man's spiritual energy; no physical or intellectual energy can achieve it.

Realization of the blessed Lord, the one Self in all, in oneself, destroys all these knots completely. Similarly, the doubts of the heart also become destroyed through realization, but not through beliefs, arguments, and discussions; and all the *saṁskāras* or *vāsanās*, that keep us chained to the sensory and genetic dimensions of life, become burned up and eliminated in the fire of spiritual experience.

This is the consummation of all spiritual practice and spiritual life, which contain a spectrum of activities like repetition of God's name, meditation, reading holy books, singing hymns and songs, and companionship with devotees of God. Through all these varied activities, strengthened by an ethical and moral life in the external context of inter-human relations, man raises his consciousness from this finite limited body level to the infinite, expansive spiritual dimension. This is the science of spiritual development and fulfillment; since all science is international and universal, this science of spirituality is universal; it cuts across all the diversities of ethnic religions, like the science of nutrition cutting across all diversities of the food habits of diverse people.

Pronunciation of Sanskrit Letters

a	(b*u*t)	k	(*s*kate)	t	no	ś	(*sh*ove)
ā	(m*o*m)	kh	(*K*ate)	th	English	ṣ	(bu*sh*el)
i	(*i*t)	g	(*g*ate)	d	equiva-	s	(*s*o)
ī	(b*ee*t)	gh	(*g*awk)	dh	lent	h	(*h*um)
u	(s*u*ture)	ṅ	(si*ng*)	n	(*n*umb)	ṁ	(nasaliza-
ū	(p*oo*l)	c	(*ch*unk)	p	(s*p*in)		tion of
ṛ	(*r*ig)	ch	(mat*ch*)	ph	(*p*in)		preceding
ṝ	(*rrr*ig)	j	(*J*ohn)	b	(bu*n*)		vowel)
ḷ	no	jh	(*j*am)	bh	(ru*b*)	ḥ	(aspira-
	English	ñ	(bu*n*ch)	m	(*m*uch)		tion of
	equiva-	ṭ	(*t*ell)	y	(*y*oung)		preceding
	lent	ṭh	(*t*ime)	r	(d*r*ama)		vowel)
e	(pl*ay*)	ḍ	(*d*uck)	l	(*l*uck)		
ai	(h*igh*)	ḍh	(*d*umb)	v	(*w*ile/*v*ile)		
o	(t*o*e)	ṇ	(u*n*der)				
au	(c*ow*)						

For information contact:
Chinmaya Mission West Publications Division
Distribution Office
560 Bridgetown Pike
Langhorne, PA 19053, USA
Phone: (215) 396-0390   Fax: (215) 396-9710
Toll Free: 1-888-CMW-READ (1-888-269-7323)